GW01605472

© IPC Magazines Ltd. 1975
SBN 85037/238/0

W-H-A-C-K! Take that! Chelsea striker Ian Hutchinson gets his full weight behind this shot towards the Liverpool goal.

£1·00

keep up with

KEVIN KEEGAN

'The rewards of life at the top'

ASK any thrusting young Fourth Division footballer what wish he'd most like granted, and I'd bet his snap reply would be: "To play for a top First Division club and my country!"

For most, unfortunately, it's an impossible dream. Yet it came true for me, Kevin Keegan, the lad from the slums of Doncaster.

I knew my performances with Scunthorpe United were attracting the attentions of talent scouts from other clubs, but all the same I could hardly believe my ears when our manager, Ron Ashman, called me aside one day and told me "one of the big outfits is going to make a bid for you, Kev."

At first I thought it was Leeds. Straightaway I began imagining myself in the famous white strip and lining-up alongside the likes of Billy Bremner and Allan Clarke.

Then I heard that my new club wasn't to be Leeds after all, but their greatest rivals, Liverpool!

Moving from the Old Show Ground to Anfield was like stepping on to the Moon. It's a different world, a world where everything is on a bigger, grander scale.

Whereas Scunthorpe had virtually no tradition at all—their highspots are reaching the Fifth Round of the F.A. Cup in 1958 and 1970, and finishing fourth in the Second Division in 1962—Liverpool had a history second-to-none in the Sixties. The Reds carried off the Championship in 1964, won the F.A. Cup in 1965, and took the title in 1966 as well as ending up losing Finalists

in the European Cup-Winners' Cup competition that self-same year.

Bill Shankly—the then-manager—one of the most respected men in the game, made it clear on the day I signed-on that he was in the process of building a team that would at least equal—if not surpass—the Sixties side—and that I was to play a key part in his plans.

I'll never forget my first experience of playing in front of the legendary Kop. The fans were even more fanatical in their support that I'd imagined. Their singing of "You'll Never Walk Alone"—the Anfield theme song—was so moving I felt inspired. I wanted to play until I dropped.

It became crystal clear to me then why visiting teams believe the Kop is worth a goal start to us in every game.

LEFT . . . Kevin kisses the F.A. Cup after Liverpool's 1974 victory over Newcastle.
ABOVE . . . Another goal in front of The Kop for Kevin (background) against Birmingham.
BELOW, LEFT . . . Kevin in action for England against Wales.

Kevin and his wife Jean at their beautiful cottage in Wales.

Kevin first wore the red of Liverpool in 1971/72. Since then, he has become a household name, winning many major honours and international caps. On the opposite page we feature two of Kevin's team-mates, Steve Heighway and goal-keeper Ray Clemence. Playing with such stars, says Kevin, makes his job much easier . . . a compliment the other Liverpool players would, no doubt, return.

What a dream debut I had in that opening match of our 1971-72 programme, scoring one of the goals that helped to beat Nottingham Forest.

And what a marvellous experience to play alongside men whom I'd only seen in action on television—the likes of Steve Heighway—SHOOT'S Most Exciting Player of the Year at the time—Emlyn Hughes, Tommy Smith, and Ian Callaghan. No disrespect to my former Scunthorpe team-mates, but the Reds seemed light years ahead on ability. I began to realise what professionalism truly means: a combination of outstanding skills, brilliant reading of a game, one hundred per cent work-rate and complete dedication.

I was amazed at how easily I slotted into the framework of the team. Being surrounded by quality players had the two-fold effect of boosting my confidence and giving me more freedom to express myself. Mates of mine on the terraces later told me I looked twice the player.

Of course, I found the opposition much harder to beat. I soon learnt that players of the calibre of Norman Hunter and Colin Todd don't naturally have off-days. It was up to me to hit such a peak that I forced them to struggle.

I also found out why our First Division is called the hardest League in the World. There are no weak teams, no chance to relax. Preparations for a match are always the same: a full training schedule, team talks and treatment for even the most minor injuries to ensure we're all in top condition when we trot out on to the park on the big day.

The chance to play against foreign club-sides is another bonus. I played abroad with Scunthorpe only once: a hectic summer tour in Spain of five matches in ten days.

To attract the crowds, the organisers billed us as the "Champions of the English Fourth Division". A real con-trick, because we'd ended that season almost propping up the table.

Apart from the sightseeing aspect—which I enjoy so much—playing abroad provides the opportunity to study the foreign stars and the different styles of the various continental countries.

My baptism in competitive European soccer came in my very first season. As Arsenal had done the "double" and were competing for the European Cup, Liverpool, as losing F.A. Cup Finalists, were drafted into the Cup-Winners' Cup tournament.

We played a Swiss club Servette Geneva in the First Round, winnning 3-2 on aggregate, and found ourselves paired with the West German Cup-holders Bayern Munich in the Second Round.

The Bayern team contained several international stars, such as Franz Beckenbauer and Gerd Muller—who'd played their parts in defeating England in the 1970 World Cup Finals—and who subsequently helped their country win the Nations Cup in 1972 and the World Cup in 1974. I felt honoured and thrilled to appear on the same pitch as them.

The Germans held us to a goalless draw at Anfield and hit us 3-1 in the second leg in Munich. They were later beaten in the Semi-Finals by Glasgow Rangers, the eventual winners of the Cup.

Another advantage of playing in our top flight is the possibility of getting the call to serve one's country. Name one Fourth Division player that's earned a full England cap!

My club showings attracted the attention of the then-England boss, Sir Alf Ramsey, with the result that I was selected for the World Cup qualifying game against Wales in November, 1972. I still treasure that old-style white England shirt I wore on my debut.

Unfortunately, I didn't exactly put on a five-star performance in our 1-0 win at Ninian Park, and although I played in the return match with Wales, which ended in a draw (1-1), I had to wait until the close season of '74 for my next game. The "caretaker" manager Joe Mercer gave me a run in the Home Championships and the successful Iron Curtain tour that followed it. Incidentally, I opened my scoring account for England with a goal against Wales and another against Yugoslavia.

I must admit I found it difficult adjusting to the England style, which is different from the way we play at 'Pool.

I'm no pot-hunter, but I get a marvellous sense of achievement when I visit my parents' home in Doncaster and look at the trophy cabinet there containing all the honours I've won—League, F.A. Cup and U.E.F.A. Cup. If I hadn't had the luck to be signed by Liverpool—and luck counts for a lot in football—I could still be a virtual "unknown" playing my heart out in the lower Divisions for a not-very fat wage packet and little glory.

As it is, I've won more honours than even some of the "greats" of English football, travelled at least half the world, played some superb football, and carved myself a very good standard of living.

My wife Jean and I have a lovely cottage in North Wales, we run two cars—a sports car for me, and a small, run-about saloon for her—and can afford quite a few other luxuries.

Liverpool pay me well—very well—but not all my earnings come directly from the game. I'm paid to endorse sports goods such as boots and footballs; I model clothes for a mail order firm; I occasionally open new shops, such as supermarkets; and I write a regular column in SHOOT.

Yes, the rewards of becoming a First Division footballer have exceeded even my wildest hopes. It's a very satisfying life.

If you don't make a habit of joining me every week in SHOOT, why not start now? I'd like that.

Kevin Keegan

Happy Arsenal fans after the 1971 F.A. Cup Final victory over Liverpool.

SUPPORTERS

West Germany captain Franz Beckenbauer with the 1974 World Cup.

CHAMPIONS

OWN GOAL

Jeff Clarke of Manchester City lobs the ball over 'keeper Keith MacRae to score—for Burnley.

A goal for England . . . Mike Channon raises his right arm in victory salute after scoring against Czechoslovakia.

ENGLAND

CUP

Sunderland players celebrate their 1973 F.A. Cup triumph against Leeds.

REFEREE

Leicester official Roger Kirkpatrick is in charge of this situation.

KEVIN HECTOR Derby County

KEN KNIGHTON
Sheffield Weds.

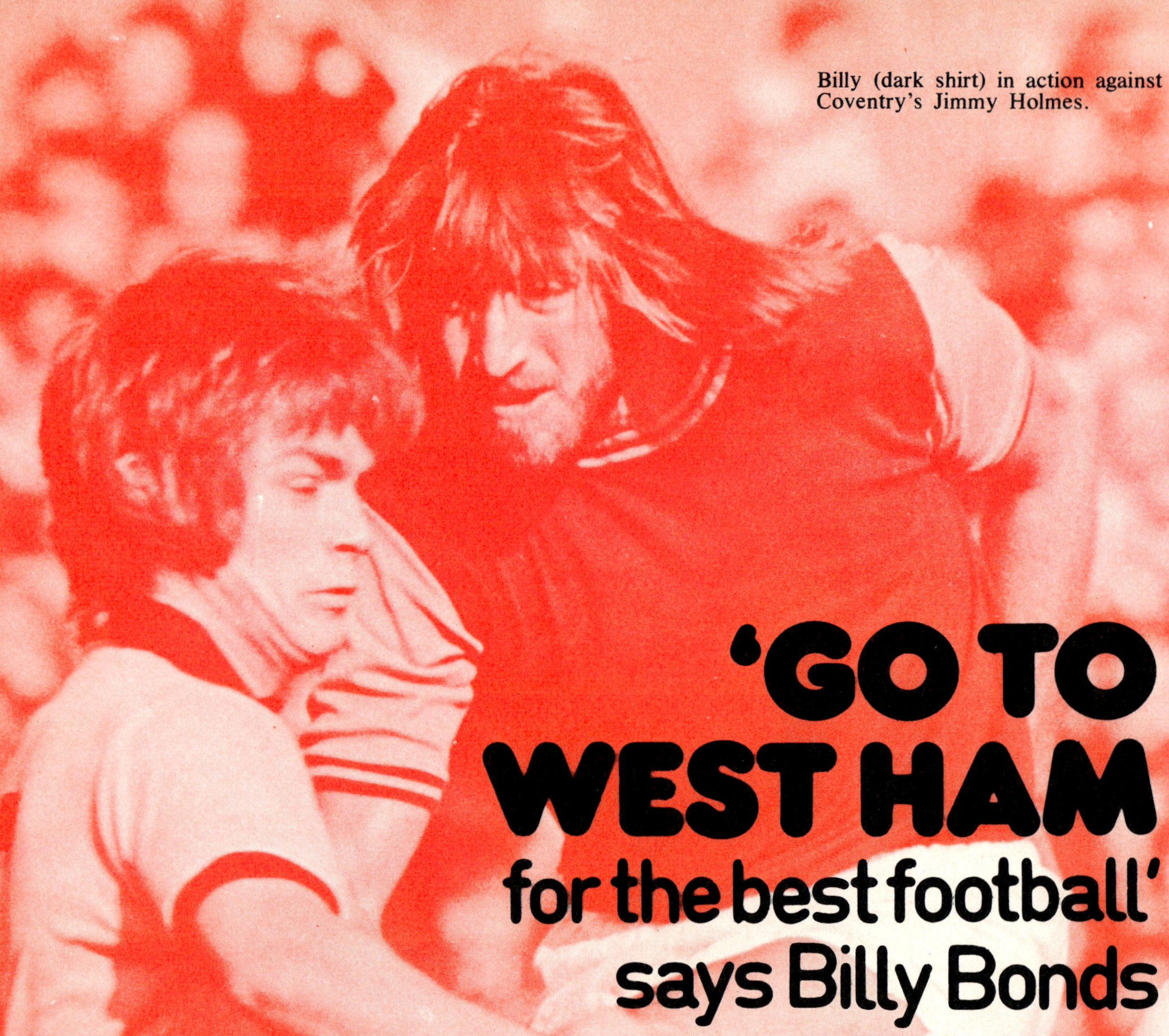
Billy (dark shirt) in action against Coventry's Jimmy Holmes.

'GO TO WEST HAM for the best football' says Billy Bonds

OVER the past six or seven seasons, London has seen its share of honours come to the First Division clubs there.

Arsenal won The Double, Spurs and Chelsea triumphed in Europe . . . but West Ham missed out on the honours. Until last term that is.

Hammers captain Billy Bonds says: "For a long while West Ham have played the best football in London yet always missed out on the pots."

Last season, of course, saw The Hammers overtake their London rivals. Suddenly, their football, which had always been entertaining, gained a new dimensions.

There was a "crazy" spell in the autumn when they scored goals almost at will, hitting Leicester for six at home and Burnley for five at Turf Moor.

"We've always had the skill," explains Billy, "but we became more physical.

"Not in the dirty sense. We did more running, working for each other, making things happen rather than waiting for them to happen.

"A lot of credit for this must go to John Lyall, who took over as team manager when Ron Greenwood became general manager.

"The results spoke for themselves and ironically it all started against Tranmere."

Ironically . . . because West Ham have an embarrassing record of being knocked out of Cup competitions by clubs from the lower divisions.

They beat Tranmere 6-0 in a League Cup replay at Upton Park, which proved to be the start of the goal-glut.

"That win gave us tremendous confidence. We were apprehensive of them, remembering our record.

"It proved that with the right attitude—and a few breaks—we could produce the goods."

Although West Ham have not been as lucky as some of their London neighbours, they have never resorted to dubious tactics and Billy is probably right in his "our soccer is best" claim.

He goes on: "Our fans like the way we play. It was sickening not to be able to string together good results, so 1974/75 and the Cup Final was a relief to all the players."

Billy doesn't say it himself . . . yet throughout the disappointments his form never suffered.

The Hammers are lucky to have such an inspiring midfield maestro, who is rarely out of the goal-charts.

"This is probably because all my career I've been used to the pressures of being at the bottom.

"With Charlton, it was usually an uphill struggle to climb away from the foot of the table, so I guess I'm accustomed to the feeling of uncertainty."

There's no uncertainty at Upton Park now. The new-look Hammers are no longer a "soft touch" as Billy puts it.

The addition of strikers Billy Jennings and Keith Robson "was wonderful for the club. Two of the best buys ever," says Billy.

Hammers fans wouldn't argue. But they'd surely put Billy, who cost only £50,000 from Charlton in 1967, at the top of the bargains list.

Spot-on . . . another successful penalty for Gerry, this time against Aston Villa.

Gerry Daly is ahead of schedule...

WHEN Bobby Charlton finally left Manchester United, he took with him a legend that will never be equalled, let alone overshadowed.

But, of course, the show must go on and The Reds seem to have found a young player quite capable of organising the midfield in the same way Bobby did for so many years.

He is Gerry Daly, a quietly-spoken Irish lad, not long past his 20th birthday.

While nobody expects him to be a second Bobby Charlton, he—and the rest of the "new" United—will be compared with their illustrious predecessors for some time.

"This doesn't bother me" says Gerry. "I realise that Bobby, Denis Law and the rest did a marvellous job for United.

"They're gone and the new lads have the same responsibility: to put United back on the top.

"I remember when I came to Old Trafford. I looked around and saw all the famous names and wondered what on earth I was doing here.

"I'm not the sort of person to be overawed for too long, though, but I'm still aware that Manchester United are more than just a football club".

Talking about not being overawed . . . Gerry certainly showed this by becoming The Reds' penalty king.

Despite having so many world-class players, United, strangely, have never had a reliable spot-kicker.

Until now. "I volunteered to take on the job before the start of 1974/75.

"My approach to penalty-taking is simple. I never believe I can miss. Touch wood, my record's been pretty good".

Gerry recalls the day when he "chickened out" of taking a spot-kick.

"I was in the youth team and missed one on a tour. When we were awarded the next one, I didn't want to know.

"So one of the other lads took it and missed. He was heart-broken, but I felt as if I, not he, had let the team down.

"Now, if I miss, I put it at the back of my mind. I'll never 'chicken out' again".

Gerry joined United in April, 1973, from Bohemians in Eire. He must rate as one of Tommy Docherty's shrewdest-ever signings.

The story goes that upon being introduced to the chairman's wife, he knelt and kissed her hand—style indeed!

"My first problem was weight and fitness, or rather lack of it.

"I could still do with putting on a few more pounds, but I'm still only 21 so I'm not too worried.

"I've been in the side for around two years, which is much better than I expected when I came here.

"I hoped to be challenging for a place by the time I was 22, so I'm delighted with the way things have gone".

So are United. They have found an all-purpose midfielder who, while not pretending to be another Bobby Charlton, is a very good Gerry Daly the First.

MIKE PEJIC
Stoke City

DREW JARVIE
Aberdeen

Go For The Double

After solving the clues in this specially compiled crossword, you can use the letters in the thick-edged squares to form the name of:— a Middlesborough full-back.

ACROSS:

(1) Top Middlesbrough goalscorer in photo C. (4 & 7)
(6) DI–AMO Z—REB (Yugoslavia).
(7) Liam —, Arsenal midfield star.
(10) T–MMY T–YLO– of West Ham.
(11) STEVE WH—WORTH of Leicester City.
(13) Mixed-up pen parts missing from GR–M—Y TOW–.
(15) Derek —, Wolves full-back in photo A.
(17) Backward animal missing from H—–ARY (European Cup country).
(18) —Patricks Athletic is a league of Ireland club.
(20) Bobby —, Aberdeen 'keeper in photo B.
(22) — Zoff. Juventus and Italy goalkeeper.
(26) — Park, Motherwell ground.
(27) Ian —, scorer of the Sunderland goal in the 1973 F.A. Cup Final.

DOWN:

(1) Surname of Footballer of the Year, 1973. Shown in photo D.
(2) — Fisher, Southampton half-back.
(3) Home of Glasgow Rangers. (5 & 4)
(4) Mixed up young goat missing from M–C–Y –ROY of Chelsea.
(5) Everton, "THE T—FEES".
(8) — City from Bootham Crescent ground. (Promoted in 1973-74)
(9) Fourth Division club whose home is Griffin Park.
(12) DAVID –OML— of Leicester City.
(14) Geoffrey —, Norwich City full-back.
(16) L–NK– PARK, Montrose ground.
(19) East —. Relegated from Scottish Div. 1 in 1973-74.
(21) —K–R PARK, Sunderland ground.
(23) The Newcastle score in the 1974 F.A. Cup Final.
(24) The way of promotion!
(25) CARD—F CITY.

Answers on Page 125

Go For The Double Go For The Double

'COOL, CALM AND COLLECTED'

—but Colin's a worrier

WATCH Colin Todd out on the park. Even in the toughest game, see how he glides confidently into a tackle and inevitably comes out cleanly with the ball. Note his anticipation, which seems to leave him at least three moves ahead of the rest of the field.

Watch Colin Todd in action and you'd think he was the original Mister Confidence. A world-class superstar without a care in the world.

Yet the Derby County defender is a self-confessed worry-guts. What's more, the man just can't help it. He HAS to have something to worry about!

He worried a fair amount when he was representing Chester-Le-Street Schools, because he got into a two-games-a-day situation (club and school) and certain local coaches told him he was burning himself out. On to Sunderland, through the junior sides, and into the first team at 17.

Interrupting the "worrying", Colin recalls a new coach who DID know what he was talking about—a former star called in to look after one of Sunderland's junior sides in which Colin played.

That coach was . . . Brian Clough. Later he was to become manager of Derby County and sign Colin Todd for £170,000.

Clough tried to iron out the self-doubt in all the players, and particularly concentrated on the young Todd. Says Toddo: "He was strict, laid on the discipline, but he made all of us feel we just wanted to play our hearts out for him."

Idolised at Sunderland, where he had nigh on 200 first-team games and where he surprisingly quickly got over his worries over replacing "King" Charlie Hurley in the Sunderland defence, Todd moved on to Derby County and admits that his worries REALLY started then.

First worry? "That the crowd would not let me forget how much money I'd cost. I knew that a lot of critics were having a snigger about it, because it was an unheard of price to pay for a straight defender. If they HAD given me the bird, it would have really hit me, and it would have brought back the early days at Sunderland when I knew I was diabolical a lot of the time . . . and really felt I'd never make the grade."

Second worry? "That I started out in midfield, and had this feeling I'd never hit it off there. I find I read the game better in the back four . . . it's not too easy to do that in the thick of the battle in midfield. Obviously I had to try it, to justify Brian Clough's faith in me—but that and the thought of the crowd maybe getting at the big-money boy . . . it was a worrying time."

But if Colin Todd worried towards the end of his first full season with Derby County, so did Cloughie and the rest of the team. They won the Championship in that 1971-72 season with 58 points, but it was a really tight finish with three clubs—Leeds, Liverpool and Manchester City—on 57 and finishing their campaigns after County had completed their own campaign.

The strain of that season told on Toddo. He says now: "We all had to spit blood for the manager, and that meant every single game. It was hard. Specially hard."

And the result was that he decided he just couldn't go on a close-season Under-23 tour with England. He said he was "too tired".

He says now: "Obviously I regret all that. It'd never happen again. But apart from the strain, there's the fact that I also hate travelling. Now that's another worry for a professional footballer, if you like! You're travelling at least every other week, but at that time Derby County was booked for a European Cup campaign, which meant a lot of extra flying. And I'm no good at flying!!

An extra worry for Toddo has been the number of judges who say (in lots of different languages, by the way) that he is destined for an even longer and more

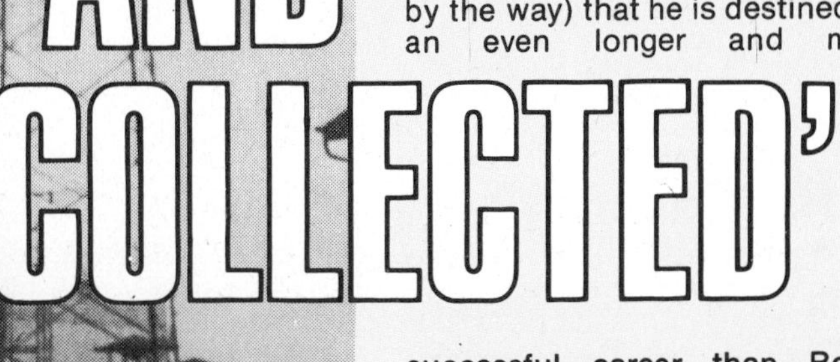

successful career than Bobby Moore. "You don't like to think of things like that", says Colin. "So many things can go wrong. A bad spell, a serious injury. . ."

But once he's out there on the park, spraying those passes with a ball he's so decisively won . . . well, Toddo just hasn't got a single thing to worry about!

AYR United striker George McLean returned from a three-month spell with Vancouver White Eagles last term and found himself temporarily banned from playing in Scotland.

The problem was that "Dandy" didn't have the necessary clearance from the Canadian F.A.

As a result of the mix-up, McLean missed a couple of games, but was soon happily back in action for Ayr.

Unfair system

NORTHAMPTON Town General-Manager Dave Bowen has no regrets at turning down the opportunity of taking over as full-time boss of Wales, before the job was offered to Mike Smith.

Says the former Arsenal and Wales wing-half: "It is a strain running an international side for a country that has such difficulty in getting players released by their clubs.

"I feel like laughing out loud when I read and hear complaints that England face the same problem. Someone has to be joking if they are compared with the plight of the three other Home countries."

SOCCER PUBS

TWO League clubs are in the public house business. Ipswich have one under the main stand called The Centre Spot and Portsmouth have The Pompey just a couple of yards from the main entrance to Fratton Park.

NEWS DESK

Compiled by PETER STEWART

HISTORIC BOOT

GEOFF Dennis, skipper of the Isle of Wight side Lud, claims an amazing record. He is convinced that he should go into the Guinness Book of Records.

While playing in a windswept match against Rookley, the Rookley 'keeper took a goal-kick which went only 20 yards.

But one of the goalie's boots came off and hit Dennis.

Said Dennis: "That must surely be the first time a player has been kicked by a boot which a player wasn't wearing at the time."

When Don Revie should have been sent off!

ENGLAND boss Don Revie was never sent-off during his 18 years as a player with Leicester, Hull, Manchester City, Sunderland and Leeds. But Don feels there are two incidents during his career when he should have been given his marching orders.

Don explains: "The first was when I played for Manchester City against Birmingham in a First Division game in 1955-56.

"A certain Birmingham player marked me the whole of the 90 minutes and some of his tackles on me were X-certificate.

"Eventually I couldn't stand

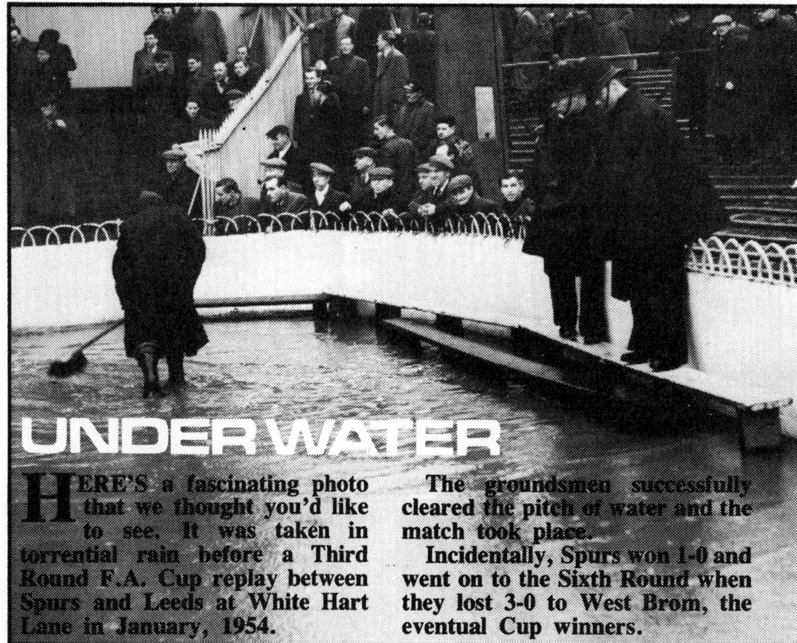

UNDER WATER

HERE'S a fascinating photo that we thought you'd like to see. It was taken in torrential rain before a Third Round F.A. Cup replay between Spurs and Leeds at White Hart Lane in January, 1954.

The groundsmen successfully cleared the pitch of water and the match took place.

Incidentally, Spurs won 1-0 and went on to the Sixth Round when they lost 3-0 to West Brom, the eventual Cup winners.

THEY certainly believe in catching them young down Loftus Road way!

Stephen Farnworth of Morden, Surrey, was enrolled last season as a fully-paid up member of Q.P.R. Supporters' Club.

Mind you, proud dad had to sign the form and cough-up the cash—young Steve was just two days old at the time!

LEEDS WIN FRIENDS

LAST season Leeds United became conscious of their image abroad. So before a European Cup-tie in Switzerland they carried out a highly-successful friends-winning campaign.

Wherever the team went in Zurich they took with them team photos and information about the club, written in the language of the country.

any more and lashed out in a rage.

"Fortunately the referee took into account all the stick I had taken and decided not to send me off.

"I was then involved in a similar incident as a Leeds player, with Tony Kay of Sheffield Wednesday.

"I retaliated after a knee-high tackle, but the ref let me off with a lecture and a booking."

Refreshing admissions from a great sportsman.

PORTUGAL'S EUSEBIO HELPED TORONTO BEAT LONDON

THREE of the game's all-time greats were in action in London last season in the World Six-A-Side Championship.

Eusebio of Portugal helped Toronto (Canada) beat a London side 13-12. Two of the London stars, Gordon Banks and Jimmy Greaves, didn't seem to mind a bit.

£1,100 to watch Bradford City play — ONCE

SOME people grumble about the cost of watching a football match these days, but it's chickenfeed compared with the price paid by a businessman who supports Bradford City.

It has cost him £1,100 to watch the Fourth Division side.

This anonymous benefactor lives in Australia, having emigrated from Bradford a number of years ago to make a million out of chemical plants.

But he has always retained his interest in City and last term signed a cheque for £1,100 for the privilege of becoming a vice-president.

His business interests take him from his Sydney home to Hong Kong for six months of the year and he can't get back to England to see his parents for more than four days.

That means his cheque guarantees him no more than one match a season.

We hope that City win the game he does manage to watch!

FIRST PENALTY

WHO, fans often ask, scored the very first penalty in a Football League game?

A League backroom boy has been doing a spot of research and came up with a player named Joe Heath.

Joe created his own little bit of soccer history on 14th September, 1891, when, at Molineux, he banged in a penalty for Wolves against Accrington Stanley.

Ireland, though, were first-off with the idea. The penalty-kick was introduced by the Irish F.A. in the 1890-91 season.

But the new rule wasn't adopted in England until the following September.

Ballet for Bristol City

IF you thought Bristol City players looked more graceful last season it wasn't surprising. For the team went on a course of ballet training to tone up their muscles and improve their co-ordination.

Here we see Ernie Hunt watching a member of the Northern Dance Theatre going through her paces. Needless to say that was one movement cheerful Ernie didn't attempt.

BRENTFORD don't often make news nowadays—but at least they must be the only League club to have a director who was a former professional with one of Europe's most famous clubs.

He's Dan Tana, now a film producer in this country — but once a player with Red Star Belgrade—who was elected in a boardroom shuffle last year.

Frannie's near miss

DERBY and England striker Francis Lee admits to missing a few shots in his career. But none of his goals that got away could be more remarkable or frustrating than the hole-in-one shot he missed when playing golf with his former Manchester City boss Tony Book and ex-team-mate Mike Summerbee.

Frannie's drive from the first tee landed just 3 inches from the hole and cost him a £500 holiday prize.

Even more fantastic was the fact that Frannie only plays the occasional game of golf and that was the first time in two years that he'd swung a club.

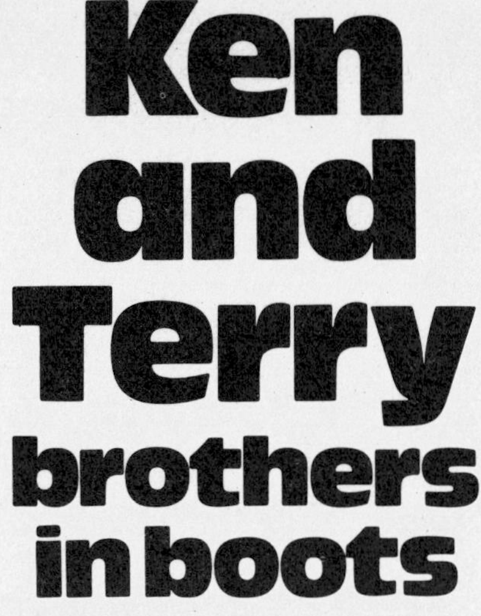

Ken and Terry brothers in boots

BROTHERLY love is forgotten when Ken and Terry Hibbitt come face to face on the football pitch.

"Once we get out on the park, Ken knows he won't get any favours from me," says Terry emphatically.

Ken nods in agreement, "That's right," he says, "When I have to play against my brother it gives the game an added incentive for me."

Terry Hibbitt of Wolves and Ken Hibbitt of Newcastle are among the few brother acts in football. And it was their father's guiding hand that pushed them forward in the tough competitive career they chose.

"Dad's enthusiasm was really tremendous," says Terry. "I cannot remember a time when Ken and I did not have a football at our feet. Dad had us practising whenever it was possible to do so."

Terry who, at 27, is three years older than Ken, adds, "Thanks to Dad I was playing in a junior team at the age of five and a half.

"By the time I was ten, Ken was in the same side and whatever the weather we always knew our father would be on the touchline, watching and encouraging us."

Terry, a natural left-sided player, began his career as an apprentice with Leeds United where he stayed for seven years before moving to Newcastle in August, 1971.

Recalling that move, he says: "It all worked out perfectly for me. Since I joined United I have gone from strength to strength. In fact, I wish I had moved earlier. I reckon those wasted years cost me an England Under-23 cap."

Newcastle manager Joe Harvey is full of praise for Terry. "I think that getting him for £30,000 must rate as my bargain buy of all time," he declares. "I don't know another player with as much vision as he has with his left foot."

Ken's professional career began with Bradford Park Avenue in the mid-Sixties. After making 13 full League appearances, he was signed by Wolves in November 1968. He made his first team debut against Chelsea at Stamford Bridge in September 1970 and scored in the 2-2 draw.

"I will never forget that game. I was very nervous about playing with so many famous players but my lasting memory is when I cracked the ball into the back of the net from Bernard Shaw's cross," he says.

Sir Alf Ramsey was quick to note the forward's promise and he came on as substitute in an England Under-23 game against Wales at Wrexham in December, 1970.

Ken says about his career: "I must admit I did have a few doubts about the wisdom of joining Wolves in the early days. I was signed from Bradford by Ronnie Allen but he left the club within two days of my arrival.

"Then I had a cartilage operation in 1969 which held me back for a long spell. I didn't think much of my prospects when Bill McGarry signed Bobby Gould and Danny Hegan in 1970. But I kept my place and have gone on from there."

The Hibbitt brothers have come a long way since father first fired their amibition with his own fanatical enthusiasm in Bradford. But the rivalry ends there.

"Whatever happens on the pitch we are always the best of friends afterwards," insist the brothers Hibbitt.

'Giddy' by name, but not by nature

"GIDDY" is the nickname given to Aston Villa full-back John Gidman by his team-mates. It could refer to his ability to leave opponents standing still, but more probably it reflects on his soccer career, which certainly has been giddy!

Rejected by Liverpool and given a free transfer to Aston Villa, Gidman has been described as an "up-to-date" full back. Not only is he an accomplished defender, but he can also turn his abilities to attacking.

"My critics say that I can't defend," says John, "but I don't think I miss all that much because my speed helps me to recover very quickly. I have found a new appetite for the game in the Midlands, and I don't hold any grudge against Liverpool. They sacked me twice, because I wasn't considered to be up to standard, but I consider I have now proved my worth."

Indeed, Gidman has developed into a very talented club player and his international career is also looking very rosy.

At almost 6ft tall, Gidman is the epitome of the classic defender, but he is realistic enough to admit that he considered his career over when Liverpool gave him a free transfer.

"It was a sickening blow to my pride," he says. "It made me all the more determined to prove myself at Villa. If I were to give advice to youngsters I would tell them to concentrate on the game and work hard. The chances have got to come if the ability is there."

However, it is Gidman's ability to surge forward in attack that baffles his critics. They maintain that he should concentrate on his defensive work and remain steadfastly at the back of the field.

Gidman does not agree.

"I started my soccer career as a midfield player and later became a winger, so it is only natural that I should want to go forward. I agree that most full-backs remain in defensive roles, but if I'm caught napping I have the necessary speed to get back in position.

"I can defend when I am called upon to do so. The fact is that I only go into a tackle when it is 50-50. Otherwise I hate selling myself and being left stranded.

"I like to 'jockey' a player and use my speed to stay with him. I reckon I'm the fastest full-back in the Football League."

A fact which Villa fans would readily endorse.

'Giddy' has lost the reject tag and now, much wiser from the experience, he is ready to make his mark for England.

Johnny Graham
AYR UNITED FC

SOCCER THE SPORT OF SHOWBIZ KINGS

IF horseracing is the sport of kings, then soccer must surely rank as the sport of showbiz.

The cries of: "There must be a joker in the crowd" and "give us a song", are becoming more and more apt as the legions of actors, actresses, comics and pop stars flood into football grounds all over the country.

London clubs have their following, with Arsenal leading the way. Not only can they boast Mike and Bernie Winters among their fans, but also disc-jockey Pete Murray, bandleader Joe Loss and Robin Chadwick, star of BBC TV's "The Brothers".

Other London clubs with star supporters include Chelsea, regularly watched by Michael Crawford of "Some Mothers Do 'Ave 'Em"; Fulham, whose Chairman is the ever-popular Tommy Trinder, and moving into the suburbs, pop superstar Elton John is very closely associated with Watford FC, and TV's top funny man Eric Morecambe is a director of Luton Town FC.

However, one has to move farther north to find the football grounds that are littered liberally with Rolls-Royces and famous faces.

Liverpool can claim the greatest following — and their showbiz legions are all as fiercely proud of the club as those assembled on the famous Kop.

LEFT . . . Mike and Bernie Winters, two regulars at Highbury.
ABOVE . . . "Some Mothers Do 'Ave 'Em" star Michael Crawford, a Chelsea fan.

TOP . . . Comedian Tommy Trinder (right) is Chairman of Fulham. With him here are Fulham manager Alec Stock and T.V. personality Jimmy Hill, a former Craven Cottage player MIDDLE . . . Superstar Elton John, who loves Watford so much he could never even consider emigrating. LEFT . . . Cilla Black is one of many showbiz personalities who follow Liverpool

Ken Dodd is a lifelong follower of The Reds, and as well as having trained with the team, he also claims to be an unofficial and unpaid scout for the club!

Cilla Black is also a regular at home matches, as is Norman Vaughan.

The club's No.1 fan is undoubtedly Jimmy Tarbuck, who was a personal friend of former manager Bill Shankly, and who claims that Liverpool has its own form of baptism.

According to Jimmy all babies born in Liverpool are submerged in the Mersey canal by their fathers. If they come out Red they are Liverpool supporters, if they end up Blue then their allegiance lies with Everton!

The latter club also attracts showbiz fans. Actress Rita Tushingham follows their fortunes, and so does top disc jockey Ed "Stewpot" Stewart.

"I first saw Everton play when I was a young lad," says Ed. "I watched them lose heavily to Chelsea and felt so sorry for them that I have supported them ever since!"

Over in Manchester there is also fierce rivalry between United and City as far as showbiz supporters are concerned.

Bill Wayne, the larger half of the comedy duo of Dailey and Wayne, has worshipped Manchester United since he was in nappies. He also has a unique link with the club. Indeed, he went for a trial at United with his schoolboy pal, Albert Scanlon.

Bill failed to make the grade, but Albert went on to enjoy a successful career with United and was ultimately involved in the Munich air disaster.

"I'm an all-round sportsman," says Bill. "When I failed the trial I went on to become a boxer and actually sparred with Rocky Marciano. It was a great moment in my life, but nothing can really detract from my love of United."

Coincidentally, Eddie Large, also the bigger half of comedy duo Little and Large, has his footballing loves in Manchester. But for him it is City that reigns supreme.

"I don't miss a home match if I can possibly help it," says Eddie, "and even now I wear a black arm-band to mourn the loss to soccer of Denis Law. He played well enough for United, but when he moved to City he became the undisputed king of Manchester."

Such fervent support has also spread to Birmingham, where comedian Don Maclean, pop star Roy Wood and several other personalities litter the terraces at St. Andrews.

It was Aston Villa that first brought to the attention of the public the strong showbiz following that soccer enjoys in this country. Indeed, a few years ago, when the club was going through a sticky patch, a consortium of showbiz stars, headed by comedian Stan Stennett, and including Mike and Bernie Winters, offered to take over the club.

It didn't happen, of course, but if proof were needed of the showbiz interest, this was it.

Staying in the Midlands, singer Vince Hill was born in Coventry and still keeps a close watch on The Sky Blues. He has often trained with the club, and his Rolls-Royce and personal luggage all display Coventry City badges.

Des O'Connor once had a trial for Northampton Town, and pop group Paper Lace share their support between the two Nottingham clubs, County and Forest.

But to return north, Roy Castle, Dickie Henderson and Les Dawson are all followers of Leeds United. Indeed, Dickie has trained with the players, and Les Dawson has used former manager, Don Revie, and Scottish fireball Billy Bremner in his TV shows!

Disguised

Impressionist Mike Yarwood has never been able to impersonate the skills of Stanley Matthews or George Best, but he has done the next best thing by joining the board of Stockport County FC as a vice-president.

However, one has to go to the far north of England—to Scotland in fact—to find the most fanatical showbiz football supporter in the country.

Pop superstar Rod Stewart rarely misses a Scotland International match, and has even placed his private jet aircraft at the disposal of friends so that they too could enjoy the spectacle of Scotland playing.

He also watches League soccer, but does admit to having trouble preventing himself from being recognised.

"I have a special disguise, comprising of long raincoat, scarf and cap, that I wear at matches," says Rod. "I also use a very old car but still I get recognised. It's incredible but I just continue going in different outfits."

So next time you are at a match, don't be surprised if you hear some better than average singing, or some topical jokes. It will probably be another showbiz star watching his favourite team in action.

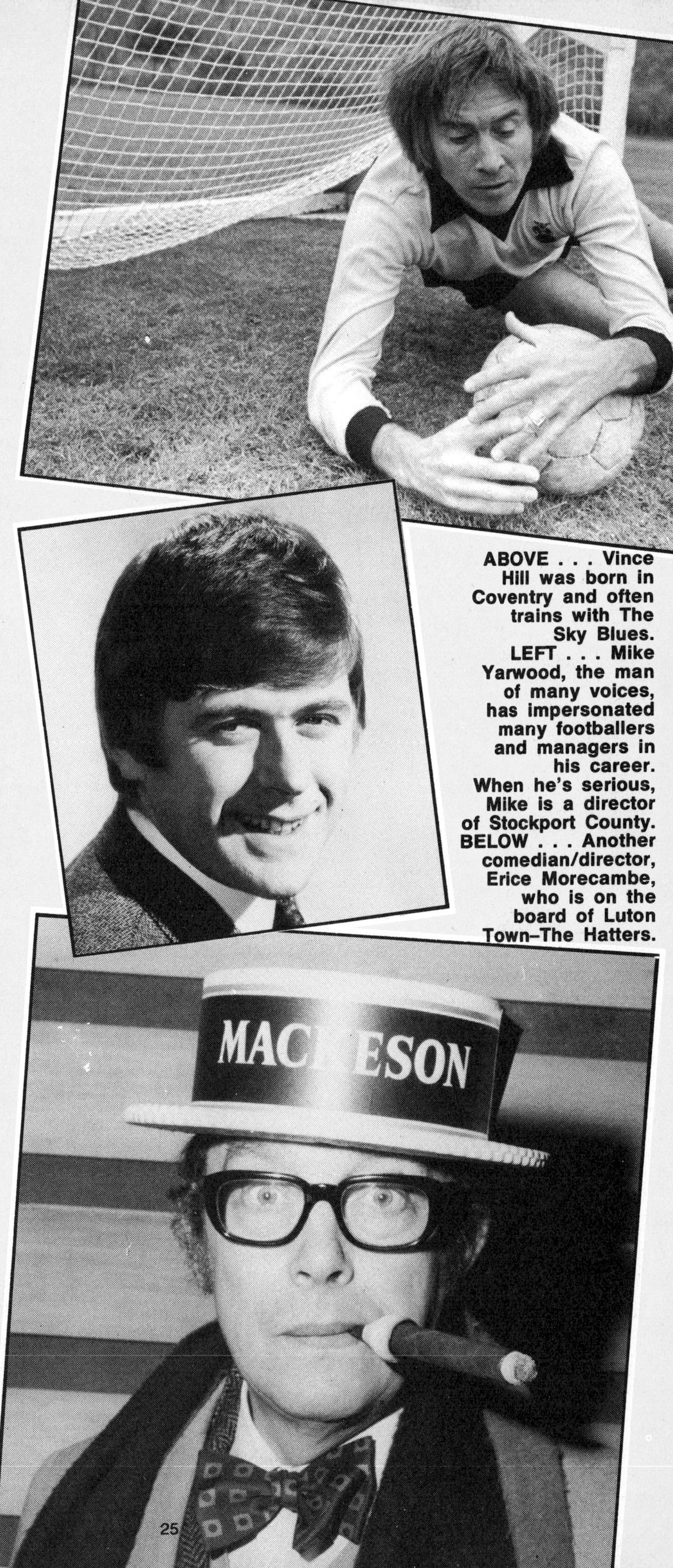

ABOVE . . . Vince Hill was born in Coventry and often trains with The Sky Blues. LEFT . . . Mike Yarwood, the man of many voices, has impersonated many footballers and managers in his career. When he's serious, Mike is a director of Stockport County. BELOW . . . Another comedian/director, Erice Morecambe, who is on the board of Luton Town–The Hatters.

Goal-keeping

by Kevin Keelan, Norwich

'COMMAND YOUR AREA'

I USED to be a left-winger with Kidderminster Harriers. One day our goalie didn't turn up. I volunteered for the job and have been between the sticks ever since.

I enjoy being a 'keeper because I have natural agility. I'm a supple person, too, and even the most strenuous exercises never present problems.

My boyhood hero was the Wolves' 'keeper Bert Williams. He was everything one could wish to see in a goalie and was nicknamed "The Cat" because of his amazing light-footed speed.

A 'keeper's job is a specialised one, and agility is the first essential. But I should stress that you can't spend an entire match leaping about all over a goalmouth. You must be prepared to come off your line.

To cut out cross-balls or smother those dangerous through passes that send a player clear and straight for goal. In a one-against-one situation such as I've just mentioned your dash to intercept must be perfectly-timed.

Never stand rooted to the goal-line. Move about the six and 18-yard areas. You must command them. By playing that way it takes a lot of pressure off your defence. You've got to be prepared to get amongst those flying boots or lunging heads and cut out the danger.

Try to convince yourself you can never be beaten. Always attempt to save every shot or header.

In a League match at Orient last season, I thought I was going to be beaten. A corner came over from my left and their number four, Peter Allen, found himself unmarked. He flashed a header down to a spot just inside my right-hand post. For a fraction of a second I felt the ball was on its way into goal, but my agility came to our rescue.

It was a save similar to Gordon Banks' effort against Pele during the 1970 World Cup Finals in Mexico. Certainly it was one of my greatest saves. A pity millions of people weren't watching *me* that afternoon!

Seriously, though, I demonstrated perfectly that I hate to be beaten. I stifled those "Goal!" cries. But that's what I'm paid to do.

Gordon Banks? What a 'keeper he was! Banksie was completely different in style from me. He seldom flung himself about a goal. He read a game so superbly. Gordon knew exactly how to narrow an angle, judge a distance. He made sure he didn't have to rely solely upon agility.

A 'keeper's job is all about angles and distances. I'm still learning!

Back-four play

by David Nish, Derby County

'WELL-TIME YOUR TACKLES'

At one time I never gave any thought as to which position I was best suited for. At school I used to play either as an inside-forward or at right-half, as the positions were called in those days.

I left school in 1966. I was on Leicester's books as an amateur at the time but signed pro. forms soon afterwards.

I played regularly for Filbert's reserves, in the same positions as at school.

I made my first-team debut just before Christmas, 1966, as an inside-forward at home to Stoke City. We won 3-2 and I scored one of our goals.

But I was soon back in the reserves, as a wing-half. It was in that position, and operating defensively, that I got a senior recall towards the end of that season. . . Graham Cross having broken a bone in an ankle.

The following term, because of an injury to John Sjoberg, the side was reshuffled and I began playing at full-back.

I used to watch Leicester a lot when I was a boy. Frank McLintock—he played at wing-half in those days — Colin Appleton, and Graham Cross — yes, he's been around a long time — were my heroes.

I didn't model myself on any of them, though. My playing style developed from within me. I let myself progress naturally.

I prefer playing at right-back. Most of my games for England have been in that position.

I'm not really left-footed. If I take on a player speeding down my left side I lose half a yard in pace through being forced to tackle him with my right foot.

To be a full-back today you need to be a midfield-man, too. You're constantly required to move upfield. The regular darting up and down a pitch demands plenty of energy. Stamina is essential for such a role.

Full-backs can't afford to make mistakes. Every pass must go to a team-mate. All clearances must get rid of imminent danger. Slip-ups can result in goals for the opposition.

Try to be a perfectionist. I do, and it helps my play. I'm lucky in being blessed with a cool temperament. It helps when an opponent tries to provoke me.

If you're in a one-against-one situation, make sure your tackle is well-timed. If it isn't your opponent is likely to get a clear run to goal.

One player I've the utmost admiration for is Leeds' Paul Madeley, who can play in just about every role. He's powerful, rarely beaten, deceptively fast, a good tackler, and has extraordinary balance.

As a full-back, he's a model of perfection. I can't pay him a greater compliment than that.

Midfield play

by Steve Perryman, Spurs

'GOOD PASSING IS ESSENTIAL'

I PLAYED at inside-forward at school because I liked that position. Our sports master believed that players performed best if they were given freedom of choice.

In the professional world, clubs tend to dictate your role. They're usually right.

Soon after joining Spurs, they decided I'd be more effective if I dropped back into midfield.

For three years I operated in the centre of the three midfield men. I was what is known in the trade as an "anchor-man".

Last season I was given the freedom to cover any one of the three positions and funnel back when necessary.

Before I made the grade in soccer my idols were Rodney Marsh—then Q.P.R.—and Johnny Haynes. Rodney to me was the great entertainer. He still is, in my opinion. A fabulous footballer, a crowd-puller if ever there was one.

I idolised Johnny because there was no better passer of a ball in the game. His accuracy over any distance was uncanny. He could weight a pass perfectly, too.

Good passing is essential in a midfield player. You must also be able to use both feet with equal effectiveness. A ball could reach you from any angle. You must be able to dispatch it in any direction . . . promptly, if necessary.

To tackle well is vital. Again situations will arise in which you're required to use both feet. And I don't mean a double-footed tackle! That's illegal.

You don't need to be a brilliant header of a ball but it will show up in your play if you're poor at it.

As most punts and goal-kicks by 'keepers usually by-pass mid-field-men you're not frequently called upon to get involved in heading duels.

A good shot in either foot is a distinct advantage, particularly from outside the penalty-box.

A player in my role needs positional sense. You can't train for it. It's born in you.

You must be able to adjust yourself to the pace of a game, soak up pressure, and move into the attack when opportunities present themselves. The midfield-man is a general.

Of today's players in that position, West Ham's Trevor Brooking catches my eye. I wouldn't say he reads a game better than me, but I feel he spots openings a shade earlier. It comes naturally to him. I'm working on getting up to his standard.

Striking

by Allan Clarke, Leeds

'BELIEVE IN YOURSELF'

I'VE always had a knack for scoring goals. It showed itself in my school days, firstly at junior level, progressing through secondary modern, South-East Staffordshire and District Boys, and finally Birmingham County Boys.

In one match—a junior equivalent of an F.A. Cup tie—I scored four goals for the South-East Staffordshire & District Boys v. Dudley Boys.

It was always my ambition to be a striker. In fact, all boys wanted to score goals in my day. I'm disappointed that lads these days want to become defenders or midfield players. Perhaps it's because goals are harder than ever to come by.

Even school teams copy the defensive methods used by League clubs and national sides.

My original hero was the old West Bromwich Albion centre-forward Ronnie Allen. I can remember seeing him in action at The Hawthorns several times. He scored so many goals. He certainly knew where the net was.

Then along came Denis Law. He had everything and was especially quick inside the six-yard box.

In my opinion, if it's born in you to be a striker you will develop that way. Practise will help, of course, but the natural ingredients must be there to start with.

Coaching will expose weaknesses and help to iron them out. But if you begin scoring goals at a very young age I feel you'll be able to do so at any level.

It's that way with me. I used to be somewhat weak with my left foot, though, being naturally right-footed. Extra coaching eventually helped to make my left foot as effective as my right.

As regards positional sense, you either have a natural aptitude for finding space or you don't.

Never hesitate when in possession of a ball. In a one-against-one situation, facing an opposing 'keeper, for instance, I know exactly what I'm going to do. In a League match last season I changed my mind and it proved costly.

It was against Everton at Goodison. I took the ball up to within a few feet of Dai Davies, and having made up my mind to go around him one way suddenly changed my decision. He dropped on the ball and I was robbed of an almost-certain goal. We lost the match, too.

I talked earlier of my bygone heroes. Today I don't have any. I'm my own idol. I honestly believe that when I'm in tip-top form there is no one to touch me. Call it arrogance, confidence, what you will, but anyone who doesn't feel he's good at his job will end up a loser.

THE MANAGER

as seen by our star cartoonist STYX

2. THE TACTICIAN

1. THE BIGMOUTH

3. THE FANATIC ON TRAINING TYPE

4. THE EXCUSE-FINDER

5. THE FLASHY TYPE

6. THE NEW MANAGER

"OUR CENTRE FORWARD'S GOT THE 'FLU —— TAKE THIS CHEQUE FOR £35,000 AND BUY ME ANOTHER –"

TRAINER

MANAGER

7. THE MONEY NO OBJECT TYPE

8. THE OVER-EXCITABLE ONE

on the ball with

BILLY BREMNER

'I'M GLAD I DIDN'T JOIN HIBS'

IT'S no secret that when I made my League debut for Leeds United against Chelsea at Stamford Bridge in 1960, I was far from happy. In fact, I was downright miserable, fed up to my back teeth with Leeds.

Despite being given that golden opportunity I was still pining to get back home to my native Scotland.

I was only 17 at the time and really not yet old enough to know my own mind. Fortunately I didn't let my heart rule my head and take the first train back to my home town of Stirling.

For about three years my attitude stayed the same. I wanted away, back across the border — and I thought, happiness.

Don Revie—who partnered me on the right-wing the day of my debut—had just been appointed manager of Leeds when I knocked on his office door and handed him my first transfer request.

I was over the moon when the club accepted it and said that Hibernian wanted me. I hoped and prayed that nothing would stand in the way of a move . . . but it did!

Apparently Leeds put £30,000 on my head and Hibs refused to pay it.

I moped about for days waiting for Don Revie to tell me that the two clubs had agreed terms, but nothing more was said. Hibs could only afford £25,000 and Leeds wouldn't accept it.

So I stayed at Elland Road and have enjoyed more than a decade of success and happiness as a result.

I've often wondered what would have become of me had I moved to Hibs. I certainly wouldn't have won

Top of page: Billy is happy he stayed at Leeds.
Centre: Don Revie with the telegrams of congratulations after Leeds' 1969 Championship victory.
Above, left: Billy, with three of his team-mates, proudly hold the Fairs Cup which Leeds won for the first time in 1967/68.
Left: The team that won the Second Division Championship in 1963-64. They are: Bremner, Reaney, Sprake, Charlton, Hunter, Bell. Front row: Giles, Weston, Collins, Peacock and Johanneson.

the honours or recognition I have at Leeds.

Naturally, I've treasured every single moment of success . . . the times of triumph which have established Leeds as one of the best clubs in the world. There are too many to talk about in detail in this annual, but I thought I'd recall the occasions of my first major honours with the club, the days when thoughts of the trials and tribulations of my early career were forgotten.

The year I made my debut, Leeds were relegated along with Luton. We struggled in 1960-61 and again the following term, when we just missed going down to the Third Division by three or four points.

It was during that campaign—in March, 1962—that Don Revie pulled the first master-stroke of his managerial career when he crossed the Pennines to sign 31 year-old Bobby Collins from Everton for about £25,000.

Many critics said at the time that wee Bobby was finished . . . over the hill. Don Revie answered them by saying: "I've bought an experienced general to organise my young players."

Well, that tremendous little Scot did organise Revie's troops and soon had us marching on to glory. From then on Leeds began to climb up and up. In 1962-63 we just missed promotion.

Stoke and Chelsea won First Division places that term, with Sunderland just missing out by finishing third.

The following season the men from Roker did go up when they finished as runners up to Second Division Champions Leeds United.

We clinched the title by winning at Swansea, Alan Peacock (2) and Johnny Giles scoring our goals.

I remember that afternoon as though it were yesterday.

In the dressing-room after the game the champagne flowed and we congratulated each other on our first achievement. But that title started a superstitution at Elland Road which didn't end until we won the League Championship for the first time six years later.

We thought it would be a good idea to parade around the pitch carrying "thank you" banners before our next home match against Plymouth as a gesture of appreciation to our fans who had supported us so magnificently.

Plymouth were in no mood to be generous, though, and we only just managed to hold them to a 1-1 draw. From then on the lads decided never to do a lap of honour again. That's why apprentices carried around the Football League Cup and Inter-Cities Fairs Cup following our success in both competitions in 1967-68.

Top of page: Celebrating League Cup victory in 1968. Above: Billy gets in a shot v. Liverpool during the match that decided the 1968-69 title. Right: Don Revie with his 1969 Manager of the Year trophy. Left: Young Billy before his League debut in 1960.

Below: Allan Clarke (hidden by no. 4) dives to head the goal which won the 1972 F.A. Cup Final.

But, as I said, that superstition ended when we won the League Championship for the first time.

So we were back in the First Division, and although I always believed that one day Leeds would be a great side, I didn't dream of the heights we would reach or that I—a player who hadn't made it easy for Don Revie—would lead them as skipper.

From then on Leeds never looked back and ended the 1964-65 term as runners-up in the League to Champions Manchester United, the side we had beaten 1-0 in the F.A. Cup Semi-Final replay a month or so earlier.

We lost 2-1 in the Cup Final to Liverpool at Wembley, knowing how close we had come to beating United to the Championship.

Leeds were three points ahead of Manchester United at Easter when they won 1-0 at Elland Road. That victory on our home ground later proved enough to give them the title on goal average.

But if Leeds were doubly disappointed in 1964-65, we had two reasons to celebrate three years later in 1967-68, when we landed the Football League Cup and the old European Fairs Cup.

Winning a Fairs Cup medal gave me a great deal of satisfaction because we had been beaten in the Final the year before by Dynamo Zagreb.

Anyhow, getting back to 1969. To reach the Final that year Leeds defeated three top Scottish sides, Hibs, Rangers and Dundee United. After opposition like that you can understand why we were so confident of defeating Ferencvaros in the two-legged Final.

Thanks to a goal by Mick Jones we won the first-leg at Elland Road 1-0, and defended superbly to hold the Hungarians to a 0-0 draw a month later in Budapest.

Our first triumph in Europe was celebrated in our hotel, along with Lord Harewood, president of Leeds and the F.A., and his two sons, who were in the party.

As the evening went on into the early hours we began a sing-song and I was delegated to act as compere to conduct the proceedings.

Everyone present, players, Don Revie, Press, even Lord Harewood had to take it in turns to sing a song. I'm not going to reveal exactly what the Earl sang, but it brought the house down. That evening demonstrated the team spirit at Elland Road. Everybody, from players to president, are part of one big happy family.

Top: Terry Cooper, Paul Reaney, Gary Sprake and Billy celebrate their 1969 Championship win. Below: The Elland Roaders beat Ferencvaros to take the Fairs Cup trophy in 1968. Right: Billy is hoisted high by his jubilant team-mates after beating Arsenal in the F.A. Cup Final in 1972.

That victory in Europe completed a unique Cup double for Leeds, as we'd already defeated Arsenal 1-0 at Wembley in March to win the Football League Cup.

Some critics said that Final was one of the worst at Wembley . . . a game dominated by defences. Well, they could be right. It took a defender, full-back Terry Cooper, to score the goal which clinched the trophy. So at long last, after being known as the best runners-up in the game, we had two pots on the sideboard in the boardroom at Elland Road.

Those successes were great, but it was the big one we wanted . . . the League title and we meant to have it.

The following season in 1968-69, Leeds were knocked out of the F.A. Cup in the Third Round by Sheffield Wednesday, by Crystal Palace in the Fourth Round of the League Cup and by Ujpest Dozsa in the Quarter-Finals of the Fairs Cup. So it had to be the Championship or nothing.

Throughout the season we had managed to keep our noses in front at the top of the First Division, even though there was one spell when we didn't play all that well.

Liverpool, Everton and Arsenal were all chasing hard on our heels, but really towards the end only Liverpool stood much of a chance of overhauling us.

Then with two matches to go we had collected 64 points; Liverpool with a match in hand were five points adrift.

If The Reds won all their remaining games, including the vital one against Leeds at Anfield, they could gain 65 points—one more than we already had.

We were fully aware of the fact that one point at Anfield would give us the title . . . and we were as determined to get it as Liverpool were to beat us.

Nearly 54,000 packed Anfield for the duel of the giants and thousands were locked out. We got our point in a 1-1 draw, but if the game lacked goals it wasn't short of thrills and incidents.

The action was furious as both sides gave their all in a battle which meant so much.

When it was all over there came one of the most moving moments of my life. As we did a lap of honour, the Kop took us to their hearts and cheered us—the new Champions — as if we were their own side.

But the season didn't end with the tension and emotion at Liverpool. Two nights later we beat Nottingham Forest at Elland Road to finish with a record-breaking 67 points. Our first title and won in record style. What more could we ask . . . what more could our fans demand?

But as you all know, and as our record since has proved, Leeds United weren't content to sit back on what we had achieved. That League Championship triumph in 1969 was just the beginning.

The following season we lost that Championship crown to Everton. Leeds finished runners up, but with only 57 points to their 66. We also lost the F.A. Cup Final when Chelsea beat us in an exciting replay at Old Trafford.

But despite those setbacks I wasn't too disappointed because I know we had given our best and you can't expect any more than that.

Success in the F.A. Cup came at last for Leeds two years later in May, 1972, when a goal by Allan Clarke was enough to beat an Arsenal side which had won the double the season before. At that moment I knew Leeds were well and truly back on top of the world.

Billy Bremner

SOCCER NEWS THAT HIT THE HEADLINES

1974 World Cup Qualifying Tournament
Hampden Park, Glasgow.
26th September, 1974.

SCOTLAND (1) 2
v. CZECHOSLOVAKIA (1) 1
Holton, Nehoda
Jordan

THE TEAMS

SCOTLAND

Hunter (Celtic); Jardine (Rangers); McGrain (Celtic); Bremner (Leeds United-captain); Holton (Manchester United); Connelly (Celtic); Morgan (Manchester United); Hay (Celtic); Law (Manchester United); Dalglish (Celtic), substituted by Jordan (Leeds); Hutchison (Coventry).

CZECHOSLOVAKIA:

Viktor; Pivarnik; Samek; L. Zlocha; Bendi; Bicovsky; Kuna, (sub. Dobias); Adamec; Nehoda; Stratil; Panenka.

REFEREE:

Herber Oberg (Norway).

West Germany here we come . . . Willie Ormond and his very merry men.

A night of glory for Bonny Scotland

SCOTLAND, glorious Scotland, emerged from the international shadows at Hampden to beat a tough Czech team and so qualify for the World Cup Finals for the first time since 1958.

It was a night of emotion and fierce tension . . . a night when a skilled, fighting Scotland refused to be shaken out of their stride by the often ruthless Czechs.

Scotland earned their passports to the Finals in West Germany with a 70th minute goal by Leeds striker JOE JORDAN, a player who had yet to establish himself in his club's side.

Jordan had been sent on as a substitute for Kenny Dalglish six minutes earlier by team-boss Willie Ormond, in a last ditch attempt to penetrate a defensive wall which had stood up to non-stop Scottish pressure.

Soon the young Leeds reserve was to become a hero to the jubilant 100,000 crowd and earn himself a place in Scottish soccer history.

Seconds after his Leeds team-mate Billy Bremner had struck a post, Jordan ran on to a centre from Willie Morgan and headed past 'keeper Ivo Viktor, who was in world-class form.

The Hampden Roar could almost be heard across the border in England as Scotland's tiny captain Billy Bremner—a giant in midfield—drove on his troops to mount attack after attack on the defensive wall which had finally been breached.

So much were the Czechs on the run throughout the game, that they were almost stunned when NEHODA put them ahead in one of their rare raids in the 33rd minute.

That goal was only a brief setback. Scotland stormed forward again and were rewarded when mighty centre-half JIM HOLTON,

Jim Holton's header makes it 1-1.

A near-miss for Kenny Dalglish.

Scotland pile on the pressure as they go for the winner.

looking every inch an international at last, headed the equaliser seven minutes later, following a Hutchison corner.

Only the brilliant Viktor, and the tough-tackling Kuna, Samek and Bendl prevented these super Scots from scoring more goals.

But if the Czechs had their heroes so did Scotland—Joe Jordan, Billy Bremner, Davie Hay, Denis Law (winning his 51st cap), Willie Morgan and Danny McGrain were all magnificent.

At the final whistle Hampden erupted. There had never been a night like it.

The return game in Bratislava a month later was just a formality for Scotland . . . almost a warm-up for the World Cup Finals.

The Czechs beat them 1-0. Nehoda was their scorer again, this time from the penalty-spot.

But, then, nobody really cared . . . Scotland had already re-emerged as an international force and were ready and able to take on the world!

Scotland's record in World Cup qualifying tournament — Group 8

Denmark 1, Scotland 4 (Copenhagen)
Scotland 2, Denmark 0 (Hampden)
Scotland 2, Czechoslovakia 1 (Hampden)
Czechoslovakia 1, Scotland 0 (Bratislava)

	P	W	D	L	F	A	Pts
Scotland	4	3	0	1	8	3	6
Czech.	4	2	1	1	9	3	5
Denmark	4	0	1	3	2	13	1

Scotland's record in the World Cup Finals in West Germany

Group 2
Scotland 2, Zaire 0 (Dortmund)
Brazil 0, Scotland 0 (Frankfurt)
Scotland 1, Yugoslavia 1 (Frankfurt)

Final Group Table (first two went through to the final stages)

	P	W	D	L	F	A	Pts
Yugoslavia	3	1	2	0	10	1	4
Brazil	3	1	2	0	3	0	4
Scotland	3	1	2	0	3	1	4
Zaire	3	0	0	3	0	14	0

Denis Law is so near.

Joe Jordan's goal puts Scotland in the Finals.

Spurs striker Mårtin Chivers reaches this corner before Everton's John Hurst can clear the danger.

RODNEY
MARSH
Manchester
City

AWARD YOURSELF TEN POINTS FOR EACH QUESTION YOU GET RIGHT. ANSWERS ON PAGE 125

2. True or false? Lubanski is shown here scoring Poland's goal in a World Cup Qualifying game against England at Wembley which finished 1-1 and prevented England from playing in the Finals!

3. At the end of the 1973-74 season, Middlesbrough were crowned Second Division Champions. Did they finish thirteen, fourteen or fifteen points ahead of the second club, Luton Town?

4. Spurs' £190,000 signing from Burnley, Ralph Coates (left), helped the club to win the U.E.F.A. Cup in 1972. A year later he was hitting the headlines again with the White Hart Lane club when Spurs won the Football League Cup against Norwich City at Wembley. But what was so significant for Ralph in the latter game?

5. In March, 1973, Malcolm Allison left Manchester City to become boss of Crystal Palace. Can you remember who replaced Allison as manager of the Maine Road club?

6. Cast your minds back to October 30th, 1974. England played Czechoslovakia in an important European Championship (Nations Cup) game at Wembley. Don Revie's men won 3-0. Mick Channon hit one of the goals . . . but who scored the other two?

7. Which two clubs would be playing against each other if the 1971-72 European Cup-Winners' Cup holders met the 1973-74 Drybrough Cup winners?

1. During last season, Mel Blyth (Southampton — above), Hugh Curran (Bolton), Billy Jennings (West Ham), Terry McDermott (Liverpool), Leighton Phillips (Aston Villa) and Terry Venables (Crystal Palace) all joined the clubs in brackets. But do you know which player moved from Watford?

9. Can you identify the Chelsea youngster (left) who made his League debut for the Stamford Bridge club, at the tender age of 16, in last season's 0-0 draw with Leicester City at the Bridge (clue: his initials are T.L.)?

8. Below is a Leeds United team group taken during the 1960's . . . but can you identify a young Freddie Goodwin—now manager of Birmingham City, of course?

10. How many goals did Don Rogers (above), now Q.P.R., score for Swindon Town against mighty Arsenal in the 1969 League Cup Final, and how many did The Robins win by?

CHECK YOUR RATING

90-100 . . . Excellent.
70-80 . . . Very good.
50-60 . . . Average

FRANK WORTHINGTON
Leicester City

WORLD~BEATERS
EUSEBIO & CRUYFF

A STAR from yesterday . . . and today's superstar. Eusebio and Johan Cruyff.

Eusebio was at his best during the 1966 World Cup Finals when the Portugal ace ended as top scorer with nine goals.

His best performance was in the incredible game against North Korea, who amazingly went into a 3-0 lead.

Then Eusebio took over, and with four goals, including a couple of penalties, helped Portugal into the Semi-Finals.

There, they met England and in one of the most exciting ties of the tournament, were narrowly beaten by the would-be Champions 2-1.

Different Talents

At his peak, Eusebio was a striker who combined power with his natural grace, a player who could take on opponents and score from 35 yards or more.

Cruyff, on the other hand, does not have such a strong shot. His strength is the way he goes past defenders with lightning bursts of speed.

The Holland captain is a goal-maker and a goal taker, a forward who makes space for others and creates it for himself.

Readers of SHOOT/GOAL voted Johan the Most Exciting Player of the 1974 World Cup Finals, a title he so richly deserved.

It was a pity that in the Final itself, Johan had one of his rare off-days and it is more than a coincidence that his team mates struggled to find the rhythm that had made them the most exciting side in the Finals.

Together

This picture was taken in 1974 before a special Europe versus South American match, organised by F.I.F.A.

It was the first-ever World Football Day and the game was held in Barcelona, where, of course, Johan plays.

Many of the world's top stars were on display and it was good to see Eusebio, even though he was past his best, line-up with Johan.

Europe beat South America in a not-too-serious game . . . but at least the lack of strong tackling enabled players like Eusebio and Cruyff to show their considerable skills.

FANTASTIC FACTS

Scored Seven—and Lost!

Denis Law (below) scored seven goals for Manchester City in a game yet they lost! It happened at Luton in the F.A. Cup (4th. Round) in 1961. City were leading 6-1, thanks to Denis Law's double hat-trick, when the play was abandoned owing to foul weather. In the replay Denis scored again but Luton banged in three, so City were out although their fair-haired Scots wizard had hit—yes, SEVEN goals in all. During his fantastic career Denis recorded hat-tricks in League and F.A. Cup games; for Manchester United in all three European competitions—and for Scotland his total of 30 goals included two "4's"—against Ireland and Norway in 1962.

Sam's 'Spectacular'

Now what about the man who scored four goals in a match yet his team only won 3-2? It was a Division 2 game between Oldham Athletic and Manchester United in 1923. Sam Wynne, 'Latics' full-back, gave his side a two-goal lead from a penalty and a free-kick, but during the second half it was two-all—and it was Sam Wynne who scored those two goals—own goals—for United. Fortunately for Sam one of his mates popped in another goal to give Oldham a 3-2 victory.

Lincoln Keep Keeper—Thanks to Fans

During the early weeks of the 1974-75 season Lincoln City persuaded West Ham to let them have their reserve goalie Peter Grotier (above) on a month's loan. The move was so successful that the Lincoln fans not only demanded their club to secure the young 'keeper's transfer but offered to collect the £20,000 fee Hammers were asking. It was an amazing situation but the transfer took place so club, player and fans were happy.

Three—Game Decider

Billy Bremner has scored some very vital goals for Leeds United but none more sensational than the one against Manchester United in the 1970 Cup Semi-Finals. The two Uniteds met at Hillsborough, Sheffield, and drew 0-0. Off they went to Villa Park for the replay but although this battle of the giants went to extra time the score sheet was still blank. For the second replay they travelled to Burnden Park, Bolton, and 8 minutes after the kick-off wee Billy Bremner rammed the ball into The Reds' net. It had taken Leeds 218 minutes to score the first goal—the only goal as it transpired—in that long drawn-out Semi-Final. But that isn't a record for the longest time before a goal was scored in a Cup Semi-Final. In 1961 Leicester City and Sheffield United were still goalless after two games, plus extra time and it was not until the 47th. minute of the second replay that the first goal came—by Jimmy Walsh, the Leicester skipper. In fact it took 4 hours 17 minutes for the tension to be broken. City eventually won 2-0. Gordon Banks and Frank McLintock were members of that side.

Cup Medals for Father and Son

In 1948 John Aston gained an FA Cup winner's medal with Manchester United. Twenty years later John Aston below, left was a member of United's European Cup winning side. No, it was not the same man. The first John Aston was a full-back, the second—his son—was a winger, and later helped Luton Town to return to Division 1 in 1974. The Cup winning story of the Johnsons and Boyles is even more remarkable. In 1899 and 1902 Harry Johnson and Peter Boyle were members of Sheffield United sides that won the Cup. In 1925 United did it again and this time the team included Harry Johnson and Tommy Boyle—sons of those former star Blades.

Brothers' Double Goal-Centuries

Arthur Rowley, who became manager of Shrewsbury Town and Southend United, and his brother John, star of Manchester United Championship and Cup winning sides, both achieved a fantastic personal record ON THE SAME DAY (Oct. 22, 1956). In the 53rd. minute of the match between Leicester City and Fulham (his former club) Arthur scored his 200th. League goal. Just 12 minutes later brother John, playing for Plymouth Argyle at Barnsley, also reached his second century of goals in League games. But although John retired soon afterwards to become manager of Plymouth, Arthur set up a record of 434 League goals.

B-Clubs Relegated

In 1971 five Lancashire clubs were relegated—Burnley and Blackpool from Division 1; Bolton and Blackburn from Division 2, and Bury from Division 3. Here's another coincidence—Colin Waldron was a member of the demoted Burnley team, and his brother Alan was with Bolton. Two seasons later that dismal record was forgotten by the Waldron family, for Colin helped Burnley to win the Second Division Championship and Alan was outstanding in the Bolton side that finished the season as Third Division Champions.

Payne-ful for Rovers

A few minutes before Luton Town were due to turn out for a Third Division match against Bristol Rovers on April 13, 1936, their centre-forward was taken ill. The only reserve present was a young half-back named Joe Payne (above) who lacked first team experience and had never played as a forward, but into the team he went. Ninety minutes later the name of Joe Payne was being flashed all over Britain. He had scored 10 of Luton's 12 goals! It was the most incredible debut in the history of first class football. He became a leading goalscorer, moved to Chelsea and won an England cap.

10-1 Slaughter

Half-time score—Spurs 10; Crewe 1! That's not fiction—it's fact. The date was February 3, 1960, and the match a replay in the Fourth Round of the Cup, after Spurs had drawn 2-2 at Crewe. A crowd of 64,365 jubilant Tottenham fans watched this slaughter of the Fourth Division side. They expected at least another ten goals in the second half but it didn't happen. Spurs slackened off and the final score was 13-2—the North Londoners' biggest victory and Crewe's heaviest defeat. That amazing game must always remain a vivid memory for Dave Mackay, then Spurs' "iron man".

Lions' Share of Glory

Is this the most fantastic record of all time? In August, 1964, Millwall began a remarkable run of 59 home League games without a defeat. It began when The Lions were in Division 4, continued in Division 3 and ended on January 14, 1967 with a defeat by Plymouth Argyle—in Division 2. In those 59 games Millwall won 43 and drew 16, with 117 goals against 33. Alex Stepney was one of the stars of that side, although he was transferred during the run to Chelsea for £50,000 in May 1966.

Finalists Barred

Nowadays the Cup Finalists are driven to Wembley in style with motor cycle police escorts. Not so in the days when the Final was played on the old Crystal Palace ground. In 1910 the Barnsley players, who were to meet mighty Newcastle United in the Final, were refused admittance to the ground! Their manager had forgotten to take with him their "official passes" and as they were mostly pit-lads, wearing long coats and cloth caps, the official at the gate could be excused for thinking they were "trying it on". After a long delay, however, an F.A. official sent out to search for the missing Barnsley team, saved the day—and the Final. But despite their late arrival those unknowns from Yorkshire held the Newcastle aristocrats to a 1-1 draw, although they lost the replay at Everton. By the way, the Geordies appeared in five losing Finals at Crystal Palace yet at Wembley won all five Finals!

3-Minute England Debuts

When Kevin Hector made his international debut for England against Poland at Wembley in October 1973 he was on the field for just THREE minutes, having been sent on as substitute. Way back in 1929 Jimmy Barrett made his first appearance for England against Ireland at Anfield but three minutes after the start he was stretchered off with a bad injury and took no further part in the game. It was his one and only game in England's colours—and it lasted just 3 minutes!

Town and Country Forward Line

Twenty years ago Swansea Town (now Swansea City of course), had an all-Welsh international forward line comprising Terry Medwin, Cliff Jones, Mel Charles and the Allchurch brothers Ivor (below, left) and Len. All were later transferred — Medwin and Jones to Spurs; Charles to Arsenal; Allchurch Ivor to Newcastle and brother Len to Sheffield United. Their combined fees totalled £115,000. Today it would be almost £750,000.

6-6 Thriller

Have you ever seen 12 goals scored in a match without either side winning? In other words—a 6-6 draw. Brian Clough will have vivid memories of such a fantastic result. It was in October 1960 when he was Middlesbrough's centre-forward at Charlton in a Second Division match and scored a hat-trick. It was a sensational game. Charlton scored first only for Brian to equalise. From then on the score went 1-2, 2-2, 3-2, 3-3, 3-4 (Clough's second), 4-4, 4-5, 4-6 (Clough's third), 5-6 and then, in the final minute Charlton made it 6-6. Brian left the field speechless!

DAVE CLEMENT
Q.P.R.

MIKE CHANNON
England

An unorthodox tackle from Burnley captain Colin Waldron . . . but Brian Kidd of Arsenal still manages to control the ball.

You can't keep up with football's Smiths and Joneses

"WHICH surname appears most frequently in the lists of players who have appeared in top class football?"

That was the question asked recently by a SHOOT reader. We agreed that it was either Smith or Jones. And after delving into the records for some hours we decided it was almost impossible to keep up with the Smiths and the Joneses of football. But the searchings brought some interesting facts to light.

Let's take the name "Smith" first. Up to the end of last year twenty-two Smiths had played for England in full internationals; nine for Scotland; two for Ireland — but none for Wales.

There was a Smith in the first-ever England team against Scotland way back in 1872 — A. Kirke Smith, captain of Oxford University in the 1873 Cup Final at Kennington Oval. Twenty years later another Dark Blue stepped up into the England limelight — G. O. Smith, who is still revered as one of the greatest centre-forwards of all time. A slim, frail-looking fellow, who played in his ordinary civvy lace-up boots, he appeared 20 times for England between 1893 and 1901, yet never played for a League club. He remained an amateur throughout his illustrious career.

In the early years of this century a number of amateurs not only played in League football but held their own in England senior sides. One of these great unpaid soccermen was Herbert Smith, a full-back with Reading, who won a host of amateur caps and had four full international caps. But Herbert Smith had one other distinction. In 1905 the F.A. decreed that players "shall wear knickerbockers that cover the knees". Herb Smith rebelled and turned out for Reading wearing shorts that exposed the knee to view. He, with several other players, many of them amateurs, were fined by the F.A. for daring to disobey. But within a year the ridiculous order was dropped — and shorts really became shorts. (How Herbert Smith would have enjoyed playing today!)

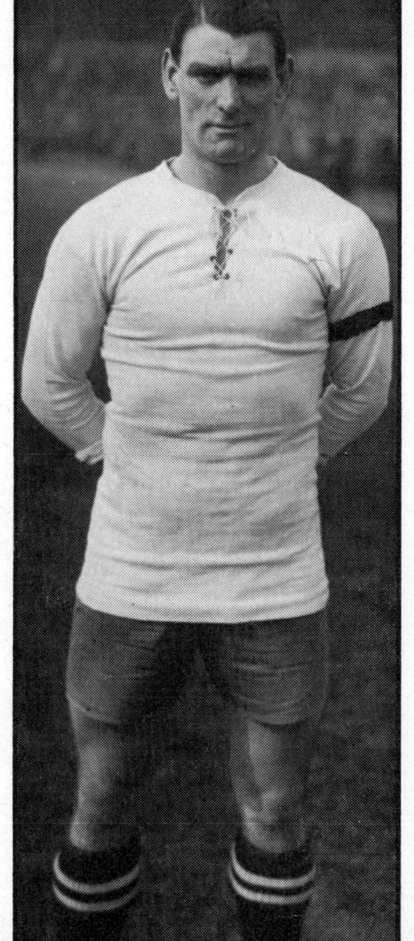

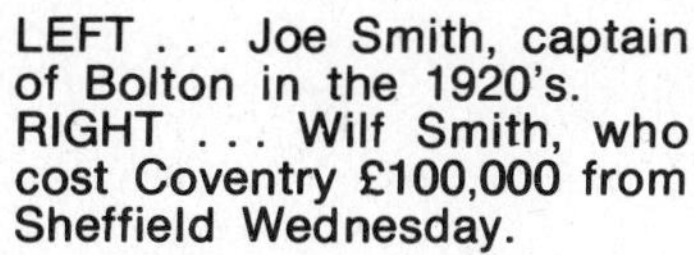

LEFT . . . Joe Smith, captain of Bolton in the 1920's.
RIGHT . . . Wilf Smith, who cost Coventry £100,000 from Sheffield Wednesday.

Smiths have played their part in every sphere of football. Take the F.A. Cup Final for example. In 1901 Spurs won the trophy for the first time and one of their goal-scorers was outside-right Tom Smith. Twenty years later Tottenham were Cup-winners again and this time their right-half was Bert Smith, a tough, rugged character, who won his England cap. To carry the coincidence further — in 1961 and '62 Spurs' brilliant "double" team was led by Bobby Smith. The big, bustling, hard-shooting, centre-forward, who appeared 15 times in an England shirt, scored in both Finals.

Bobby wasn't the only Smith to score in a Cup Final. Huddersfield Town fans — at least the older ones — will recall with pride their former idol, W. H. "Billy" Smith. The lanky, long-striding left-winger with a cannonball shot, was the star of the greatest Huddersfield team of all time — the first side to win three League Championships in successive seasons (1924-25-26) and were runners-up in 1927 and '28, and won the Cup in 1922. That Final, at Stamford Bridge, will never be forgotten. With 89 minutes gone the two sides — Huddersfield and Preston North End — were still goalless. Then Billy Smith was fouled in the 18-yard box. "Penalty" signalled the ref, and with no sign of nerves Billy Smith placed the ball on the spot and then cracked it into the net. It was the winning goal.

Billy Smith played in two more Finals, 1928 and 1930, but was unable to add to his winner's

Liverpool's Tommy Smith.

medal. Before he retired in 1934 he had played in over 500 League games for Huddersfield. His son, Conway Smith, also a winger like his Dad, played for Huddersfield and Queen's Park Rangers before injury brought his career to an end.

In 1923 — the year of the first Wembley Final — Bolton Wanderers won the trophy with TWO Smiths in their attack: Joe, their popular skipper and inside-left, and John Reid, Scottish international centre-forward, who had previously won a Scottish Cup medal with Kilmarnock. J. R. scored one of the two goals by which Bolton beat West Ham in that 1923 F.A. Cup Final. Three years later Joe Smith led Bolton to their second Cup triumph and J. R. was also a member of that team. In later years Joe became manager of Blackpool and led them to three Cup Finals — as losers in 1948 and '51 and then to victory in the 1953 "Stanley Matthews" Final. He certainly brought fame to the great footballing Smith family.

A rather remarkable Scottish scoring record was set up by a Smith. In 1927-28 Ayr United were promoted to the First Division and the man who made it possible was Jimmy Smith, their centre-forward, who hit 66 goals in 34 games. The record still stands. Big Jim later played for Liverpool and Bristol Rovers.

Rangers had a goalgetter named Jimmy Smith in the 1930s. He was the Ibrox strike-leader in several Championship and Cup-winning sides and like his record-breaking namesake played for Scotland. Many years later another Jimmy Smith hit the Scottish headlines with Aberdeen and in 1969 was signed by Newcastle United for £100,000.

Bobby Smith (left), a regular goalscorer for Spurs and England in the 1960's.

RIGHT . . . Bryn Jones, who won 20 international caps for Wales.

Among the modern generation of Soccer Smiths is another member of "The £100,000 Club" — Wilf, stylish full-back who played in the 1966 Cup Final for Sheffield Wednesday and four years later moved on to Coventry City. But the Smith family would not be complete without hefty, tough-tackling Tommy, Liverpool's "King of the Kop", who surely would be a universal choice for captain of a team of the greatest Smiths in Soccer history.

Now from the Smiths let's turn to the "Jones Boys", and as you would expect, the majority of them are Welsh-born, Forty three players named Jones have worn the Welsh crimson shirt in internationals; three have played for Ireland; 7 for England but none for Scotland.

Way back in the 1870s we find the first Jones Boys in Welsh teams — and several of these grand old men of the past played for Druids, the first club to be formed in North Wales. But the development of the game in South Wales really put the Soccer Jones Boys on the map. Swansea can be justly proud of its Jones family. The first Swansea Town player to be capped for Wales in 1920 was Ivor Jones, a brilliant little inside-forward, who later moved to West Bromwich Albion, for a fee of £2,000 — and that was big money in those days! Ivor had two brothers, both midget marvels, Emlyn, who played for Everton and Southend United, and Bryn, perhaps the greatest of the three. He began his fabulous career with Wolves and in 1938 created a sensation when he was transferred to Arsenal for £14,000, a record fee at that time.

Some years later Swansea produced two more members of the same Jones family — the brothers Cliff and Bryn. Cliff, of

One of Wales' most exciting players . . . winger Cliff Jones (heading).

course, became one of the greatest wingers in the game when he joined Spurs in 1958, for not only did he play 68 times for Wales but was an outstanding member of the famous Tottenham "double" team. Spurs also took another fine winger from Swansea Town — Willie Jones, who won caps with both clubs soon after the Second World War. Now there is Barrie Jones, midfield genius, who started with Swansea and has since starred for Cardiff City.

In the 1920s Cardiff City introduced a young wing-half to the League game named Charlie Jones. Later he made his name with Nottingham Forest and Arsenal.

Everton once had TWO centre-halves named Jones — Jack and Tommy. In 1939 both were capped — Jack for England and Tommy for Wales, but their greatest regret was that they were never in opposition for their countries.

Bristol Rovers have caused reporters and commentators some consternation during recent seasons with THREE Jones Boys in their team — Bryn, ex-Cardiff City; Philip, also from South Wales, and Bobby, born locally. The problem becomes even more complicated when Rovers play Bury, with George Jones; Walsall with Stan Jones and Notts County with Mick Jones — no relation to the Mick Jones, Leeds United's £100,000 strike-leader.

Only three players named Jones have won Irish caps but two of them were brothers — Jack, a fine centre-half who played with Linfield and Hibernian, and Sam, a wing-half, who will be remembered for his grand work with Blackpool. In 1934 the Jones brothers played side by side for Ireland against England.

Several very great players named Jones have worn England shirts — Herbert, a classical style full-back of Blackburn Rovers; Billy, a grand Liverpool centre-half of the '50s, and, of course, Mick, the £100,000 striker of Leeds United fame. And there will be more for the name of Jones is famous in football.

ABOVE . . . Bristol Rovers have fielded three Joneses at times! Here's Bryn, who joined them from Cardiff City.

BELOW . . . Leed's Mick Jones (light strip) isn't a Welshman. In fact, he has played for England.

Crossword

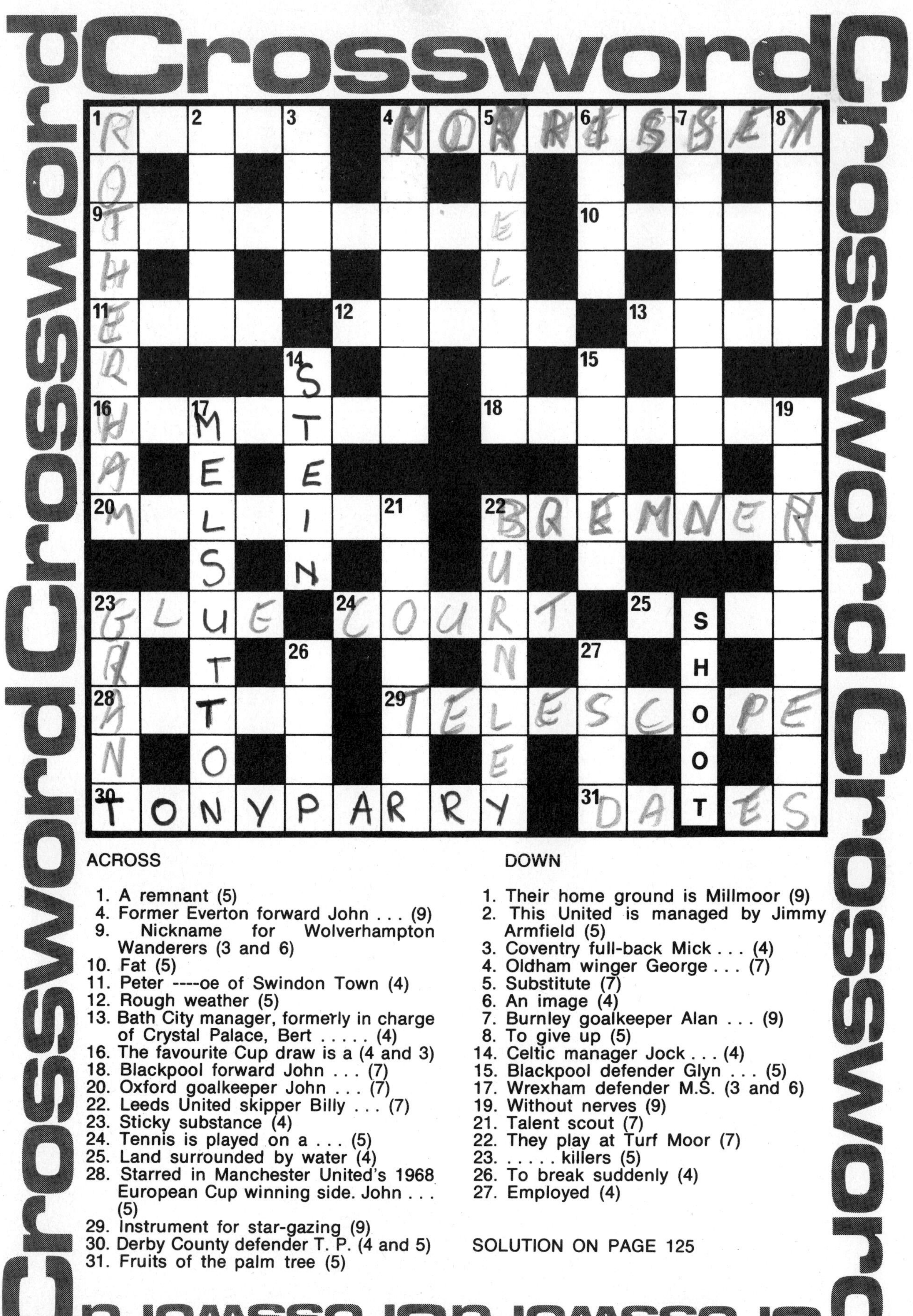

ACROSS

1. A remnant (5)
4. Former Everton forward John . . . (9)
9. Nickname for Wolverhampton Wanderers (3 and 6)
10. Fat (5)
11. Peter ----oe of Swindon Town (4)
12. Rough weather (5)
13. Bath City manager, formerly in charge of Crystal Palace, Bert . . . . . (4)
16. The favourite Cup draw is a (4 and 3)
18. Blackpool forward John . . . (7)
20. Oxford goalkeeper John . . . (7)
22. Leeds United skipper Billy . . . (7)
23. Sticky substance (4)
24. Tennis is played on a . . . (5)
25. Land surrounded by water (4)
28. Starred in Manchester United's 1968 European Cup winning side. John . . . (5)
29. Instrument for star-gazing (9)
30. Derby County defender T. P. (4 and 5)
31. Fruits of the palm tree (5)

DOWN

1. Their home ground is Millmoor (9)
2. This United is managed by Jimmy Armfield (5)
3. Coventry full-back Mick . . . (4)
4. Oldham winger George . . . (7)
5. Substitute (7)
6. An image (4)
7. Burnley goalkeeper Alan . . . (9)
8. To give up (5)
14. Celtic manager Jock . . . (4)
15. Blackpool defender Glyn . . . (5)
17. Wrexham defender M.S. (3 and 6)
19. Without nerves (9)
21. Talent scout (7)
22. They play at Turf Moor (7)
23. . . . . . killers (5)
26. To break suddenly (4)
27. Employed (4)

SOLUTION ON PAGE 125

A feature on international debuts

Arsenal Star made his England debut at 39!

SOME people nowadays believe rightly or wrongly, that a top footballer is *over* the top at thirty.

The great Bobby Charlton brilliantly soldiered on for quite a long stint — but even he was only 32 years and 8 months old when he played his 106th, and last, full England international.

Another "great", Bobby Moore, was six months past his 33rd birthday when he set the existing record with his own 108th full game for England.

But these were rare exceptions to the general rule.

Contrast their cases with that of Leslie Compton — fellow-Arsenal star, and elder brother of famous England cricketing hero Denis — who earned his FIRST cap six years older than Charlton's last.

True, "Big Les" was something a bit out of the ordinary. His whole international career was necessarily brief — making his debut against Wales on 15th November 1950, and then filling the centre-half berth once more against Yugoslavia exactly seven days later, before bowing out for good — but he was remarkably in his 39th year at the time.

Thirty years earlier, Billy Meredith was nearly 46 when he played his last official game for Wales — but he was a very seasoned and experienced international.

No one else has ever made a DEBUT for one of the Home nations — possibly for no other major footballing country, either — at Compton's age.

At the other end of the scale is Terry Venables. By 1964, at the tender age of 21, he was already the proud possessor of England caps at all five levels — Schoolboy, Youth, Amateur, Under-23, and Full.

ABOVE . . . Terry Venables was capped by England at every level. BELOW . . . The great Jimmy Greaves in action against Wales.

ABOVE . . . Leslie Compton earned his first England cap when he was almost 40! He won only two full caps in all.

ABOVE . . . George Best made his debut for Northern Ireland aged just 17 years and 328 days.
BELOW . . . Bobby Charlton as a Manchester United junior in 1953. Bobby won over 100 England caps.

Bobby Charlton's first goal for England, against Scotland.

Ironically, Terry won his last full cap only six weeks after his first — adding fuel to some peoples' theory that, perhaps, you can rise right to the top too soon.

Against that, though, one can point to the fact that, of those players listed in the "Top Ten" table opposite, only Kernoghan and Edwards ultimately made less than twenty full appearances.

And Edwards had already played 18 games for England before his tragic death, at the age of 21, in Manchester United's Munich air disaster.

Otherwise, this truly magnificent young player's final total would surely have been nearer, or even past, the century mark.

Jimmy Greaves didn't do too badly, either — 20 years and 9 months old when he scored his 100th First Division goal; still under 24 by the time he'd notched his 200th; plus scoring on his England debut three months after his 19th birthday.

Go back a bit farther to the days when all teams both had wingers and scored plenty of goals — this chap once hit 33 First Division goals in a season for Arsenal from the extreme left flank — and there's Cliff Bastin.

England's "wonder-boy" of the decade before the war played League football (for his home-town Exeter) at 15; and had won every major honour the game then had to offer — playing for his country, and winning both League Championship and F.A. Cup-winners medals — by 19.

Like Greaves — who scored 357 League goals; all in the First Division — Bastin also lasted well till war cut short his career, and even came back after it to play a handful of games for Arsenal in his late thirties.

And who can ignore the claims of that supreme entertainer Denis Law?

Scotland's youngest-ever full international in 1958 . . . "King" Denis pressed on to play his 55th game, and so become his country's most-capped player, in the World Cup Finals 16 years later.

And how about England's three centurion cap-holders — Bobby Moore (108), Bobby Charlton (106), and Billy Wright (105)?

Moore was 20, Charlton 20, and Wright 22 — though the latter's debut may well have been delayed while waiting to take his bow in the very first full international when normal football was resumed after the war.

But how long does it take, as a general rule, to make the full international grade these days?

That's a question virtually impossible to answer as individuals, and circumstances can vary so much.

Clearly, because of the far less a choice of players from whom to pick, an Irish or Welsh youngster has a proportionately much better chance than his English opposite number.

As, of course, it's always been. Another glance at our "Top Ten" list shows that all but two come from Wales or either side of the Irish border.

And, when it comes to England, it does seem on balance that the "entry-age" into the full international team — if not, perhaps, the larger international squad — is lengthening.

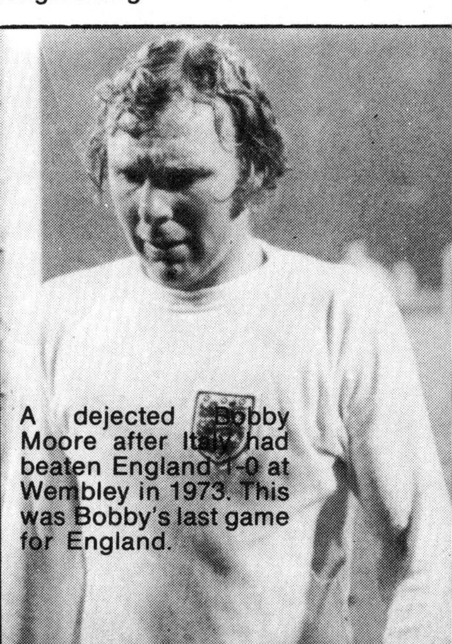

A dejected Bobby Moore after Italy had beaten England 1-0 at Wembley in 1973. This was Bobby's last game for England.

Pele won his first cap for Brazil against Argentina in 1957 aged 16 years and nine months.

With something around the 22/23 mark as a pretty fair bet nowadays, the chances of a teenager making his debut are growing slim.

One of the reasons may indirectly have been the introduction, in 1954, of the then new Under-23 category of internationals.

Before that, if a young potential star was considered good enough to be tested, he *had* to be tested in the heat of full international battle.

Many failed, some succeeded — but, at least, they got their chance there. Now there is the lesser category in which to try out their talents first.

No one can fairly complain about that — in fact, on balance, it's proved a first-rate innovation — with just one proviso.

For there's a theory, right or wrong, that an Under-23 starlet tends to be regarded as just that — and no more — until he IS 23.

No one, for instance, could seriously have doubted the abilities of Mike Channon in his "mini-international" trials — but the fact remains he had to play all nine of his Under-23 games before he gained a full international cap.

Tony Currie played ten of his 13, too; while both Allan Clarke and Colin Bell followed the same general pattern.

It's obviously easier to gamble on a promising youngster or two in an Under-23 game.

But in modern full internationals, even the so-called friendly ones, the pressures are so great, and so much prestige at stake, that all team managers tend to be playing safe and waiting longer — perhaps sometimes too much longer — before "blooding" the latest lads to catch their eye.

Teams in the 1974 World Cup Finals, for instance, averaged getting on for a couple of years older than their counterparts of 1966.

The rare youthful Greaves-type genius which just can't be held back will still emerge internationally in the future, even if less so than in the past.

"TOP TEN" YOUNGEST CAPS — Britain and Eire

NORMAND KERNOGHAN (Belfast Celtic) .... 17 years/80 days
(Northern Ireland *v.* Wales : Belfast : 11th March 1936)
JIMMY NICHOLSON (Manchester United) .... 17 years/256 days
(Northern Ireland *v.* Scotland : Glasgow : 9th November 1960)
GEORGE BEST (Manchester United) .... 17 years/328 days
(Northern Ireland *v.* Wales : Swansea : 15th April 1964)
JOHN CHARLES (Leeds United) .... 18 years/71 days
(Wales *v.* Northern Ireland : Wrexham : 8th March 1950)
DUNCAN EDWARDS (Manchester United)............... 18 years/183 days
(England *v.* Scotland : Wembley : 2nd April 1955)
GRAHAM MOORE (Cardiff City)................................ 18 years/224 days
(Wales *v.* England : Cardiff : 17th October 1959)
GARY SPRAKE (Leeds United).................................. 18 years/231 days
(Wales *v.* Scotland : Glasgow : 20th November 1963)
DENIS LAW (Huddersfield Town)............................. 18 years/236 days
(Scotland *v.* Wales : Cardiff : 18th October 1958)
ALEX ELDER (Burnley).. 18 years/343 days
(Northern Ireland *v.* Wales : Wrexham : 6th April 1960)
JOHNNY GILES (Manchester United)....................... 18 years/361 days
(Eire *v.* Sweden : Dublin : 1st November 1959)

The great Pele was only 16 years and 9 months old when he made his debut against Argentina in July 1957 — but Brazil's youngest-ever international, Dorval, played in the same match at 15 years and 10 months.

Two other very young foreign internationals — both 16 — were Brichant (Belgium, 1914), and Bickel (Switzerland, 1935).

Johan with his Datsun sports car outside the Barcelona stadium.

'Europe will fear my club'

by Johan Neeskens, Barcelona and Holland

SHOOT: Johan, what is it that makes Barcelona one of the great European clubs?
NEESKENS: It's something you notice when you arrive at the club for the first time, as I did, back in the 1974 close season. Other clubs have it as well, like Arsenal, and Manchester United, and Benfica, and AC Milan. For want of a better word, they have . . . poise. There's something special about their self-assurance, their tradition, their approach to all aspects of the game.
SHOOT: Were you overawed by what you found?
NEESKENS: I suppose so, at least when I first got off the plane. There was a posse of photographers and press men, but somehow we seemed to be whisked through customs, past all the barriers, and into the plushest car I'd seen in my life, and off to a magnificent lunch, then out to the stadium.
SHOOT: Tell us about the Gran Estadio.
NEESKENS: Well, it holds 90,000 people, and that work is under way to extend it to 120,000. It doesn't hold all that many under cover, but then the weather is comparatively mild and dry here, so that isn't so important. The facilities are quite magnificent, vast dressing-rooms with dozens of baths and a treatment room that would do justice to a modern hospital, plus lounges for the players and their friends — even a private chapel.
SHOOT: Describe a typical week with Barcelona.
NEESKENS: There's no such thing as a typical week! But we play, as you know, usually on Sundays, which means that we do only light training on Saturdays and none at all most Mondays, although if you need treatment you have to come in. All the field training is with a ball, and we go pretty well flat out every full day. In Holland Feyenoord were usually reckoned to be the fittest team, but when they played against us in a European Cup-tie last year, we ran them into the ground.
SHOOT: All the same, Johan, that doesn't sound like Barcelona have discovered anything that will revolutionise the game . . .
NEESKENS: Perhaps not, but they have taken the worry out of the player's life as far as they possibly can. For instance, at Ajax I even used to drive to the ground wondering if anyone would have pinched my car space: in Barcelona, everything is laid on so efficiently that one just gets out and hands the car keys to a commissionaire who drives it away and parks it. It's the same when we travel — there's always half a dozen officials to look after our every need. We always fly if it's at all possible, because the railway is not too efficient in Spain; and when we arrive at an airport all the formalities are taken care of so there are virtually no hold-ups.
SHOOT: Except from autograph hunters, we suspect . . .
NEESKENS: Oh, they're the same wherever you go, the only difference at Barcelona is that it's souvenirs they want, not just autographs. I've caught kids trying to unscrew parts of my car, and outside our flat taking bits off the front door.
SHOOT: And the press cause you a few problems, too, you've claimed in the past.

Johan Cruyff at a Press conference after a match. Johan now speaks Spanish fluently.

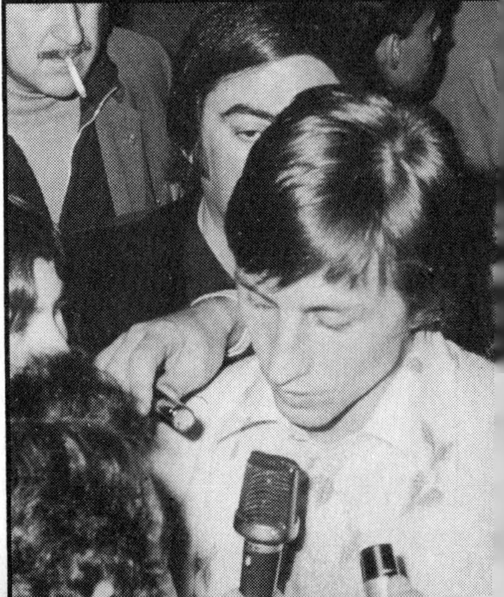

NEESKENS: Yes, but don't misunderstand me — I've nothing against the press — they've got a job to do like everyone else. But at Barca there seem to be about a dozen of them full-time on the club every day. You give one interview, and they all want an interview. The phone rings incessantly, and however many times I change the number, the secret is out within a week. The press seem to get into the dressing-rooms without any problem both before and after the game, which takes a bit of getting used to after the fairly strict regulations at Ajax. I sometimes think they'd like to interview me every time I clean my teeth!

SHOOT: Still, seriously, the club does have a great tradition . . .

NEESKENS: I only realised just how great when we celebrated our 75th anniversary last autumn. Every section of the club had a special international match — hockey, athletics, basketball, baseball, rugby, with the football team playing East Germany. The whole match was shown live on Spanish TV, but nearly 60,000 still turned up to see what was, after all, only a friendly.

The Barcelona ground and part of the luxurious changing rooms.

SHOOT: Was that the sum total of the celebrations?

NEESKENS: Far from it. One of Barcelona's oldest fans, 82-year-old Joan Miro, who is one of the greatest artists in Spain, designed a special commemorative poster which has been printed in tens of thousands. There was a special symphony concert in the Santa Maria del Mar Cathedral, when the orchestra played one of Pablo Casal's best-known works, and invited his widow to attend, arranging for her to fly in all the way from Puerto Rico. The cathedral was packed, with 8,000 people seated, and even more, 15,000, went to the pop festival held in the club's main sports hall the following week.

SHOOT: Barcelona really play a full part in city life, it would seem . . .

NEESKENS: They certainly do. You know, the club held a competition to find a theme-tune for the spectators to sing before matches, and there were nearly 20,000 entries. The winning song was tried out for the first time when we played West Germany, and, take it from me, it's not bad at all. The following day more than 6,000 supporters went on a hike up the side of the Montserrat, that's the symbolic mountain of Catalonia, the province in which Barcelona is the capital. They visited the Monastery of the Black Virgin on the mountainside, and raised a collection for them of more than £1,000 on the spot. The whole month of celebrations was rounded off with a banquet.

SHOOT: Before Rinus Michels took over as manager, Barcelona went for 14 years without winning the Spanish Championship. Is there a danger of this ever happening again?

NEESKENS: I doubt it. On the one hand, you have Michels, who is a genius — he picked the club off the floor in the 1971-72 season, when they looked even in danger of relegation. They finished third the following year, and in 1974 they won the Championship. But Michels could never have done it without Johan Cruyff, and he could never have signed him without the financial skill of the president, Don Costa. Barcelona had spent so much on players in the early Sixties, when I'm told we had almost two complete teams of internationals, with players like Czibor and Evaristo and Villaverde from half a dozen different countries! Even then they got beaten by Real Madrid in the big games, and eventually the bubble burst, and the club almost went into bankruptcy. But all that's different now: Johan paid for his transfer within a year, just by what he put on the gate, and nowadays there's plenty of money to buy new players.

SHOOT: Some of the more unkind critics have said that despite having you and Johan Cruyff, Barcelona still aren't a great team by any means — what do you say to that?

NEESKENS: I am sure Rinus Michels knows better than anyone that you cannot buy a team, you have to work patiently over the years. He hasn't been helped by the Spanish F.A. regulations, which have prevented the Peruvian forward Hugo Sotil and the Argentian Heredia from playing their full part in League matches. But what with our Spanish internationals Asensi, Rexach, Marcia, Miguel and de la Cruz, plus the Brazilian national captain Mario Marinho, I still think we have a team that Europe will fear.

The men who bring you ...

FOOTBALL ON RADIO

FOOTBALL supporters rely more than ever on the radio for coverage of the country's greatest sport. They have instant soccer at their finger tips.

For as little as £2 you can buy a transistor radio and listen to reports of a dozen matches any big football day or evening and a second half commentary on one of them.

SHOOT went behind the scenes at Stamford Bridge last season to record for our readers the effort that goes into a big match night, and allows the B.B.C. to entertain millions all over the world.

As Chelsea's giant £2 million stand rose into the West London skyline, the B.B.C. were allowed a say in the planning of the stadium.

The next time you walk along the wide passageway at Stamford

Bridge, glance at a door with the words B.B.C. on it.

In it is the hub of the radio broadcasts from Chelsea.

As the stand was built, telephone lines were laid in steel pipes in the structure to connect that little room with the outside world.

That room is the control centre of the whole operation and on the night we visited Stamford Bridge Freddie Sullivan was the engineer in charge.

Freddie has been with the B.B.C. since 1937 and a touch of his hand gave us contact with commentators at six other League Cup matches that evening.

Well-known radio voices like Bryan Butler, Maurice Edelston, Larry Canning and Stuart Hall came to us over the air.

At Stamford Bridge was producer Roger MacDonald, commentator Peter Jones, who was aided by Mike England, better known as Wales and Tottenham's former centre-back.

Check calls for volume with each man was given the o.k. by engineer Freddie Sullivan.

Freddie linked the second-half commentary with flash reports from the other matches.

But even the end of the match was not the end of work for the B.B.C. men at Chelsea.

Both Peter Jones and Mike England recorded pieces for the early morning sport programmes. Once again Freddie Sullivan was the man who had to make sure that it reached technical perfection.

Even then the long night was not over. The SHOOT team joined Mike England in his chase down the many flights of stairs to yet another piece of B.B.C. planning. Across from the dressing-rooms they have had built a special interview room.

In this room crammed Mike England, producer Roger MacDonald, Peter Jones, two members of the SHOOT staff and the man who was the cause of the interview — Alan Hudson, Stoke's star capture from Chelsea.

It gave Mike England a chance to prove he is as good at asking questions as he was at stopping opposing strikers on the pitch.

As Alan Hudson said his farewells, it was time for the producer to check with Freddie Sullivan that his recording was up to standard and at long last the B.B.C. team could head for home.

So next time you turn or push in a switch for your 'instant football' spare a thought for the men who put so much into bringing it to you.

The B.B.C. commentary team in action (far left). Producer Roger MacDonald checks on the telephone as Peter Jones (centre) and Mike England bring you all the thrills of the match. B.B.C. Engineer Freddie Sullivan (above photo, seated) checks his equipment. (Left) The view of the action from the radio position in the stand at Stamford Bridge. Player-turned interviewer Mike England holds the mike (below) as he chats with Alan Hudson after the match at Chelsea.

NOBBY
SEEN THESE JOKE PENS?
THEY'RE FILLED WITH INVISIBLE INK
AND THE WRITING DISAPPEARS AFTER A FEW MINUTES
I COULDN'T RESIST BUYING ONE FOR A CHRISTMAS PRESENT
... AND GUESS WHO I SENT IT TO?!
ROWE

soccer as I see it

ALAN BALL

I DARESAY many of you reading this article want to be a professional footballer.

From the moment I was born, that was my ambition. I lived, breathed and talked football. For me, there was no other way I could earn a living.

It wasn't easy. There were plenty of setbacks, but if you *really* want to succeed in soccer, you must never be disheartened when people say: "Sonny, you're not going to make the grade."

I was told that on quite a few occasions. In my mind, though, I was adamant that I WOULD make the grade and with my father's advice to guide me, I'm proud to say I have fulfilled just about all my boyhood dreams.

My very first club was Wolves. I was 14 at the time and with my headmaster's permission, I used to play for one of their junior sides.

In those days, I lived just outside Bolton and the journey to the Midlands took three hours each way.

Unfortunately, my headmaster put a stop to this because he

'I played two matches a day!'

claimed my studies were suffering and anyway, I wasn't playing for the school team!

By then, I was almost 16 and Wolves promised me that when I left school, they would sign me on as an apprentice.

In the meantime Bolton, my local club, approached the school and asked if I could play for them.

This suited me as it was nearby . . . which was just as well.

On Saturday mornings I turned out for my school, and in the afternoons I played for the Bolton "B" team.

Around this time, I sat my G.C.E. examinations and, not too

A young Alan Ball in his Blackpool days.

Alan with his father, who has been the biggest influence on his career.

surprisingly, failed the lot.

As far as I was concerned, I didn't need G.C.E.'s for the job I wanted!

My dad and I went along to see Bolton one day to see about the possibility of signing on as an apprentice-professional.

This was the crunch . . . and Bolton decided that I was too small. They let me continue in the "B" side, but as I had left school, I needed some sort of an income.

The manager at Bolton then was Bill Ridding — and I don't know for sure, but I bet my dad had a few choice things to say to him.

Anyone who said his son wasn't going to be a footballer was no friend of my dad's!

This was during the summer and we decided to take our holidays to get over the disappointment.

Needless to say, I packed my boots with my swimming trunks!

One day, my dad decided to take me on a mystery tour, boots and all.

I had absolutely no idea what he had in mind. When we got near Bloomfield Road, home of Blackpool F.C., the penny dropped.

My dad arranged for me to play in a trial game the following day at the Squires Gate training ground.

The manager there was Ron Suart and when I shook his hand that sunny morning, little did I realise just how much I would eventually owe to this man.

The next 24 hours were murder. I couldn't think of anything but the trial . . . it went over and over in my mind a million times.

The day seemed like a year and while I wasn't nervous, I just wanted to get on with it.

My dad gave me all the confidence in the world. He told me I was going to be a great player, that sooner or later some club would realise it.

I believed him and I can't say how much I owe to his enthusiasm and dedication in my early days. Even now I still learn something from him every time I see him.

So . . . the time came for the trial. There were quite a few other lads at the ground.

It was a strange sort of atmosphere. We all wanted each other to do well, but not at each other's expense, if you see what I mean.

I played less than half-an-hour in the game. Then Ron Suart called me off.

I was sure I'd done well, but wondered why he'd taken me off. I soon learnt.

"You'll do, Alan. I'd like you to join us as an apprentice-professional."

Alan in action for England at Wembley.

In his famous Number Eight shirt for Everton.

Ron's words were magic. I could hardly believe my ears — at last, I was on the first step of the ladder.

We went into his office to sort out the details and it was then that we realised that I was still on Bolton's books.

My heart turned over. There was no need to worry. A quick phone call sorted things out and I was a Blackpool player, on a salary of, if my memory serves me correctly, £6 per week.

My dad could do no more . . . he'd paved the way for me, now it was up to me.

It wasn't too long before I was in the first-team. I made my debut against Liverpool, at Anfield, too — and after a few months I had made a place for myself in the Blackpool line-up.

Ron Suart went out of his way to help me I don't think I was the easiest of players to handle, but he understood me and I can never thank him enough for his guidance.

In those days, 'Pool didn't enjoy the best of results. Most of our time was spent fighting against relegation to Division Two.

I loved every minute of it, however. All my life I'd wanted to be a professional and when it came, it was even better than I'd hoped.

I was still with Blackpool when I helped England to win the World Cup in 1966 and it was with great reluctance that I asked for a move. Blackpool were a fabulous club and I couldn't fault them in any way.

Some said I was being disloyal, but the only reason I wanted a move was ambition.

I wanted to play for a top team . . . I wanted to be involved in Cup Finals and European competitions.

Frankly, much as I liked life at Bloomfield Road, I couldn't see my dreams being realised there in the near future, so I decided that in order to further my career I had to have a change of club.

It was a decision that I hated. I talked for hours with my dad and we decided that to keep my career moving forward, I'd have to get away.

Of course, Everton made a record bid for me and after discussions with Harry Catterick, their manager at the time, I signed.

I was sad to leave Bloomfield Road. They'd given me my chance, but in fairness I like to think I gave 100 per cent all the time.

Alan and Q.P.R.'s Stan Bowles in a midfield tussle.

I became Britain's costliest footballer with a £110,000 price tag.

Soon after the transfer, my thoughts drifted back to the days when people said I wouldn't make the grade . . . I was too small . . . not good enough.

It hurt at the time, yet it made me even more determined to succeed.

The votes of "no confidence" motivated me and with my dad behind me all the way, I managed to prove the doubters wrong.

I'm not an isolated case. Perhaps even YOU have been told the same.

Forget it. have faith in yourself, believe in your ability — and, you never know, you might play for England one day, just as I did.

LIFE in the North-East just couldn't be better, and believe me if I didn't like it up here I wouldn't stick around.

Life in Geordie-land is much more personalised than it is down south. It's easier to get to know people and I've found that business often seems to overlap into your social life.

Yes, that's right, I said business. Apart from my goalscoring job with Newcastle United, I also own a fashion boutique called simply—Malcolm Macdonald—For the Exclusive Man!

I'd like to think we were exclusive as well, for my partner, Alan Owen, and I don't believe in dealing in bulk. Instead we prefer to cater for more individual tastes specialising in suits and jackets.

All our clothes are expertly tailored and although neither of us knew very much at all about the trade when we started, we have learned fast. End of commercial!

Music Fan

Sometimes I wish there were 25 hours in every day and eight days in a week. I'm so busy that most nights I don't arrive home until seven, but then I do enjoy the life I lead.

My business calls understandably limit my social life and already I've given up golf. I used to play quite a lot but now I've given my clubs to my younger brother who, at 13, seems to be making more use of them than I ever did.

Even so I still find time to go out for a quiet meal

Malcolm in action against Leeds' goalkeeper David Harvey and (below) in his boutique.

'I lead a busy life — on and off the field'

says Malcolm Macdonald

with my wife Julie. We both enjoy all types of food and I especially like to vary my grub—Indian, Italian, Greek or plain old English, it's all the same to me.

When I'm out with Julie it sometimes gets a drag when people continually recognise me and ask for autographs, but the way I look at it is that once people stop noticing me then I'm on the way down.

Apart from eating out, I also like to listen to music. I have a fad about my stereo system and although I would never class myself as a hi-fi fiend, I do like to unwind by listening to folk or rock music.

I'm also a keen driver and enjoy getting behind the wheel of my Alfa Romeo. It is practically jet-propelled and I get a real kick driving it.

You'd think all that would be enough to keep anyone occupied—but not Malcolm Macdonald.

On a Saturday when we're playing away I host a pre-recorded radio programme for Radio Newcastle that is transmitted at two o'clock in the afternoon. It's not just restricted to football either as I also play three or four tracks from my favourite LP's and interview a well-known personality.

It all adds up to a hectic life . . . but I'm not complaining and wouldn't change it for the world.

Denis Law and George Best.

Shay Brennan, David Herd, Alex Stepney, Pat Crerand and above all George Best, who like the immortal Duncan Edwards was destined to become one of the greatest stars in soccer history.

George Best wasn't in the team which won the F.A. Cup in 1962-63, but another post-war Old Trafford hero was—the King himself, Denis Law. Brought from Torino in July, 1962, for a then record transfer fee of £116,000.

With the added strength of John Connelly, an England winger from Burnley, came more triumphs, the League Championship in 1964-65 and 1966-67. The following season they were pipped for the title by Manchester City, but don't mention that around Old Trafford.

Even then, United were to overshadow their close rivals, by becoming the first English club to win the European Cup Final—their 50th game in European competition.

The Final at Wembley against Benfica established United as one of the greatest of all time. Inspired by the words of Matt Busby and the skills of George Best they came back after extra-time to beat the Portuguese 4-1.

It was the greatest moment in Matt Busby's life—his crowning glory. Soon after he was awarded with a knighthood for his services to football.

After that triumph United failed to maintain their position at the top. Sir Matt decided to hand over team affairs to a younger man—and in 1969, 31 years old Wilf McGuinness, the club's assistant-manager, took over the tough task of taking United on to more glory.

Unfortunately, McGuinness wasn't given enough time, or maybe power, and 18 months later he was sacked.

United struggled in the League and even had to fight hard to avoid relegation. McGuinness was replaced with 42 year-old Frank O'Farrell, and for a while it seemed as though United were on their way back. But in December, 1972, the former Leicester boss was also dismissed and Tommy Docherty gave up his job as Scotland team-manager to step into the hot seat at ailing Old Trafford.

Nobody really envied The Doc. Sir Matt had achieved so much that he was very difficult to replace—as McGuinness and O'Farrell had already found out to their cost.

Like O'Farrell, The Doc spent money in an effort to keep United in the First Division.

George Graham arrived from Arsenal for £120,000, Alex Forsyth from Partick Thistle for £100,000, Jim Holton from Shrewsbury for £80,000, Lou Macari from Celtic for £200,000 and in March, 1974, Jim McCalliog from Wolves for £60,000.

Despite those new signings and Docherty's inspiration, United were relegated in 1973-74. The First Division mourned their passing, the Second welcomed them with open arms.

Storm of Controversy

Gone from Old Trafford were George Best, who had quit football after a storm of controversy; Nobby Stiles, Bobby Charlton and Denis Law. Four stars that can't be replaced overnight.

It seemed United were down and out once again. But with the same spirit and enthusiasm of United's ancestors The Doc said before the start of the 1974-75 campaign: "Don't weep for Manchester United. Out of the ashes of last season will rise a team good enough to take on the world."

To reinforce this claim Docherty bought £200,000 striker Stuart Pearson from Hull City and sold Brian Kidd to Arsenal. It proved a master stroke.

United started 1974-75 with a 2-0 victory away at Orient raced to the top of the Second Division and stayed there.

Stuart Pearson, Sammy McIlroy, Gerry Daly, Jim Holton, Jim McCalliog, Stewart Houston, Brian Greenhoff and Lou Macari became the new names at Old Trafford as they again made United a feared and respected force in British football.

The dawn of a new era of success for Manchester United could be on the horizon.

Stuart Pearson (left) scores yet another goal.

LEFT TO RIGHT . . . Tommy Docherty, Jim Holton and Alex Stepney.

TOM WALLEY
Orient

ALAN
STEVENSON
Burnley

Middlesbrough's

FEW clubs have made as big an impact on Division One following promotion than Middlesbrough in 1974/75. After winning the Second Division Championship with ease, they carried on where they left off and within a few months had even topped the table. Their form last season owed much to the commanding defensive play of captain Stuart Boam, a blond giant in the centre of the defence. On the park, Stuart is a fine example to his team-mates, his no-nonsense approach makes him one of Division One's best defenders . . . ask Birmingham's Kenny Burns, who lost out on the heading duel pictured left. At home, Stuart the family man relaxes with his wife Valerie and daughters Lynne and Lorrene in their house not too far from Ayresome Park. Baby Lorrene doesn't seem too keen on football, but Lynne certainly likes a swinging—and tickling!—time.

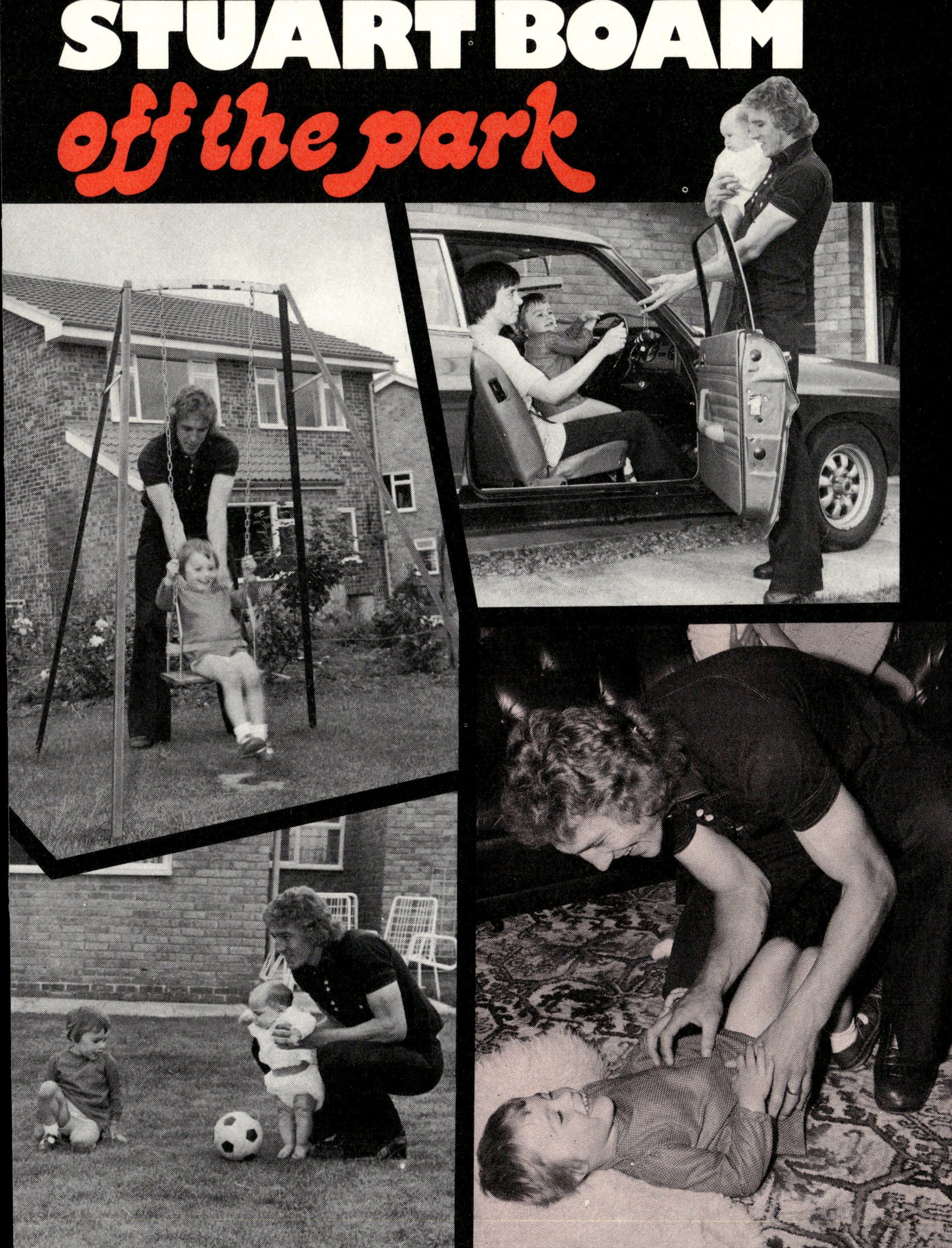
STUART BOAM
off the park

BILLY DEARDEN
Sheffield United

FRANK'S IN CHARGE!

WEST HAM'S exciting form in 1974/75 was due mainly to their go-for-goal style that had opponents reeling. Full-back Frank Lampard had a splendid season, commanding in defence yet still finding time to break forward and score a few goals. This picture shows Frank in command as he marshalls his defence at a corner-kick.

Meet Muhammad Ali — the players' choice

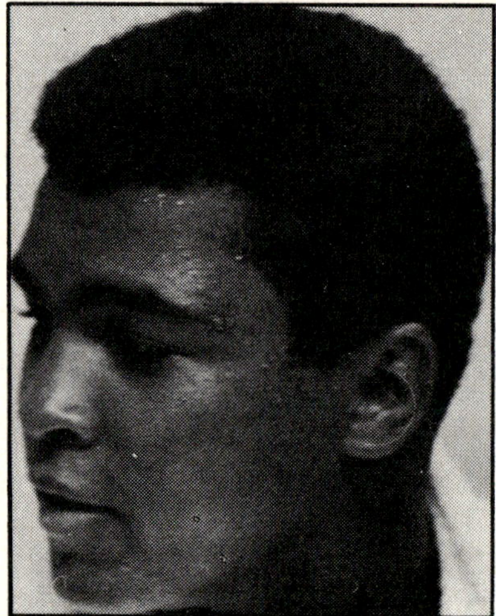

Which person in the world would you most like to meet? FOCUS ON feature in SHOOT/GOAL asks this question and a lot of footballers have replied: Muhammad Ali.

One of the Ali Fan Club in professional soccer is Geoff Salmons of Stoke City (left). So we asked Geoff why he, among so many, chose the world heavyweight boxing champion.

'He's out of this

SAYS GEOFF SALMONS OF STOKE CITY

"Everything about Muhammad Ali I like and admire" replied Geoff. "He's just out of this world, isn't he? He's the greatest. No doubt about that.

"Not only do I admire his boxing skill but also I like his personality. Whatever he says, people listen to him. When he appears on television, I can't drag my eyes away and I listen to every word he utters.

"Yes, Muhammad Ali is the one person in the world I would like to shake hands with and have a chat."

BLABBERMOUTH, Louisville Lip, Black Magician, The Greatest. . . . . .are some of the names given to Cassius Marcellus Clay who is now known throughout the world as Muhammad Ali.

Ali reigns supreme as king of all the heavyweight boxers.

When he "whupped" George Foreman in eight rounds at Kinshasa, Zaire, in October 1974, Ali was rightfully restored as the World Heavyweight Champion after six frustrating years off the throne.

At the age of 32, he proved that he could still "float like a butterfly and sting like a bee".

He made the world well aware that he was no ordinary mortal. He had almost everyone coming round to his long-held view that he was the greatest of them all.

What sort of man is Muhammad Ali? There are many facets to his character. He can be brash and arrogant, gentle and modest. He can be extremely witty and yet bore some people with his repetitive phrases.

Ali is a poet who does know it. His verses trip patter-like from his famous lips.

Asked by Oxford University to become an honorary professor of poetry, Ali declined the invitation because he was too busy training and wrote back:

"Pay heed my children and you will see
Why this is not the time for your university
It's not the pay although that's small
But I had to show the world I can still walk tall."

Before he fought Joe Frazier for a second time, he boasted:

"I'm gonna help the energy crisis by putting his lights out."

Ali admits:

"When you're as great as I am, it's hard to be humble."

Asked at a Press conference, "Was your pride hurt when Ken Norton broke your jaw?", Ali replied:

BELOW
Ali—then still Cassius Clay—was almost knocked out at Highbury in 1963 when Our "Enry . . . Henry Cooper . . . sent the Louisville Lip sprawling to the canvas. Unfortunately for Henry, Ali recovered and went on to win the fight. How ironic that the footballers' hero was almost knocked out at Arsenal.

"No. My jaw was hurt."

His poetry won't ensure him of immortality, but he has certainly achieved everlasting fame with his fists.

He is a Muslim and believes in the life-style set out by Elijah Mohammad, leader of the sect known as the Black Muslims. Ali preached as a minister of the sect but was expelled when he returned to fighting in 1970.

punching power but he astounded them by producing a right hand punch that no one thought he had to knock out Sonny Liston in the first minute of the first return of their return bout.

Ali has always confounded his critics ever since he became World Heavyweight Champion at the age of 22 years and 39 days.

Born in Louisville, Kentucky, Ali got above average marks as a

Some of Ali's Fan Club of Footballers

Bryan King
Ray Kennedy
Alan Woodward
Stan Bowles
John Richards
Keith Eddy
Peter Hindley
Geoff Palmer
Quintin Young
Colin Viljoen
Ray Graydon
Gordon McQueen
John Marsh
Jim Holton
Alan West

***LEFT* Ali gives someone a verbal blasting! *RIGHT* Ali, 1974 style, complete with umbrella, arrives at Heathrow for a short visit to England.**

He's mischievous. After losing to Joe Frazier, he led a spartan life in a wooden house in the mountainous wilds of Deer Lake, Pennsylvania. He called his shack "Uncle Tom's Cabin" because it appealed to his sense of humour.

"Uncle Tom" is the derisory deadly insult that black Americans reserve for someone of their own race who adopts a servile attitude to the white boss—and not even the worst of Ali's enemies could accuse him of that.

After regaining the world title, Ali told reporters: "That wasn't me knocking out Foreman. That was Allah."

But he went on as Ali the Arrogant to say: "Never again say I'm going to be defeated. Never make me an underdog until I'm 50."

Years ago critics thought they had spotted a weakness in Ali's boxing. They said he lacked

high school scholar of the classics. His father was a songwriter — from whom presumably he inherited his love of poetry.

Boxing as an amateur, Ali quickly got to the top. He won a gold medal as a light heavyweight in the 1960 Rome Olympics, knocking out a Belgian and outpointing a Russian, Australian and a Pole.

The story goes that he was so fast early in his boxing career that after flicking off the switch in his bedroom he could get between the sheets before the light went out. Certainly none of his opponents could catch him.

Ali admits that he was at one time a sucker for a left hook. British Champion Henry Cooper floored him with his famous "'ammer"— a left hook; Joe Frazier made him groggy with one when he lost the world title by being out-pointed over 15 rounds; and Ken Norton broke his jaw with another.

But Ali has never been knocked out. Up to regaining his title last year (1974), he had been beaten only twice—by Frazier and by Norton against both of whom he later took ample revenge.

Above all Ali is a superb entertainer who can draw crowds by the pure magnetism of his personality He is totally unpredictable as a fighter. Sometimes he goads his opponents into making mistakes. He drops his guard and lets them hit him—just to show that he can take their punches.

Ali lies back on the ropes, covers up and lets his opponent punch himself out as he did with Foreman in Zaire's 100,000 capacity national stadium. He always seems to win the pyschological battles.

Often he has baffled his opponents with rapid changes of pace. At times he has appeared sluggish and tired but then he has suddenly sprung into fast action, dancing around and not allowing one punch to land on him.

Ali can be a killer in the ring. He can also show mercy. He rarely stops talking—and most of what he says makes good sense.

Certainly there will never be another world champion like him.

Down goes George Foreman—and Ali retains the World Title.

WHEN Rangers and Celtic meet, the action is always thick and fast. Our picture shows some of this action as Rangers' striker Derek Parlane skilfully avoids a sliding tackle from Celtic defender Jim Brogan.

There is nothing quite like an "Old Firm" game, which has an atmosphere all of its own. This excitement spreads from the terraces to the players . . . hence the action-packed local derbies in Glasgow.

CHANGE OF COLOURS FOR BLUES STAR

BIRMINGHAM fans know Howard Kendall as a non-stop midfield grafter who never gives less than 100 per cent. Our photographer caught a new-look Howard at home with his wife Cynthia . . . although it's unlikely he'll ever turn out at St. Andrews in this "strip"! Cynthia is wearing a Football League shirt Howard won a few years ago. Howard himself has a change of colours—blonde to be precise. It's enough to give Birmingham fans the blues!

KEITH FEAR
Bristol City

LEFT . . . The old Spurs favourite Ted Ditchburn, who played in more than 400 League games for the club.

Do 'keepers last longest

PLAYERS come and players go but goalkeepers go on for ever . . . well, so it would seem judging by the incredible longevity records of many of the game's greatest 'keepers. We are not suggesting that goalies live longer than their contemporaries in the other team positions, just that they seem to last longer in the top rankings before packing up and handing over the job to younger men.

Proof of this can be found in the fact that many of the club "most appearances" records have been set up by 'keepers—Spurs for instance. Between 1946 and 1959 Ted Ditchburn played in 418 League games for the North Londoners. That figure might have been much higher but for the cessation of League football during the war, for Ted joined the club as a junior in 1937. Now the Spurs' record has passed to another 'keeper, their handsome Irishman Pat Jennings, who can also add 48 games with Watford before moving to Tottenham in 1965. Before he ends his fabulous career Pat could smash every record in the book.

Among modern 'keepers Jim Montgomery has earned a high reputation for his consistent dependability. He made his League debut for Sunderland in 1962 and less than eleven years later had set up a new appearances record for the Roker Park club with 420 games. Since then, of course, he has shattered the old record of 419 by Ned Doig beyond recall. Ned, Scottish international and one of the greatest goalies of his time, reigned supreme for 14 seasons (1890-1904) and helped Sunderland to four League Championships.

We find further proof of our contention that goalkeepers last longest in the fact that some of the appearance records set up years ago are still unbeaten, including that of Notts County. In 1904 lanky 6ft. 5in. Albert Iremonger made his first appearance for County in Division 1. Twenty-two years later, having passed his 40th birthday, he had

BELOW . . . One of the most stylish goalies of yesteryear, Harry Hibbs, the former Birmingham star.

reached the colossal total of 564 League games, including one amazing run of 223 consecutive matches. Even then he refused to "fade away" and spent a couple of seasons with Lincoln City, but right to the end of his career he remained one of the great crowd-pullers with his colourful character and entertaining antics on the field. He thought nothing of racing from his goal to take throw-ins or even dribbling up the field, yet he was a brilliant 'keeper—his fantastic record proves that.

One of Iremonger's contemporaries was "Tim" Williamson, who was Middlesbrough's No. 1 from 1902 until 1923 and played 561 League games for the club, a record that remains to this day. Of course that figure, like Iremonger-'s, might have been even greater for their careers included the war years 1915-19 when there was no League football. Tim Williamson, by the way, was the first Middlesbrough player to earn an England cap in 1905.

Then there was Jerry Dawson who will never be forgotten at Burnley. During his 21 years at Turf Moor he made 530 League appearances, a club record that may never be beaten, at least not by a goalkeeper. Local-born Jerry played twice for England and won a Championship medal in 1921, but the only time when he was absent through injury he missed the 1914 Cup Final. Burnley won and his deputy (one of eight who must have despaired of ever getting a chance) enjoyed the hour of glory that should have been Jerry's.

You may be surprised to know that Everton's appearances record is also held by a goalkeeper—Ted Sagar, who kept vigil in the Goodison net for more than 24 years. He joined the Blues from Hull City in 1929 and began an amazing run of 465 League games ending in 1953. During that time he won two League Championship medals, a Cup winner's medal and 4 England caps.

Birmingham fans will need no reminding that two of their greatest players of the past were long-service 'keepers. From 1925 until the war-break in 1939 Harry Hibbs was regarded as the most stylish and accomplished goalie in the country. He appeared in 360 League games for Brum and 25

LEFT . . . Bert Trautmann broke his neck playing for Manchester City in the 1956 F.A. Cup Final.
BELOW . . . Frank Swift, who died in the Munich disaster.

Peter Bonetti is one of the longest-serving goalies in the game. He made his Chelsea debut back in 1960.

for England. After the war his successor became almost as famous. He was Gil Merrick who set up a club record with 486 League appearances in the space of 14 seasons and played 23 times for England in 24 consecutive games. After vacating the Birmingham goal in 1954 he became the club's manager. His record is still intact.

Manchester City's "man-of-most-matches" record was held for more than ten years by Bert Trautmann, the former German paratrooper who, after a spell in a Lancashire prisoner-of-war camp, was persuaded by City to settle in Britain. From 1949 to 1964 he guarded City's goal in 508 League games, setting a new club record. He also played in the 1955 and 1956 Cup Finals. Big, blond, breezy Bert was City's hero in the second of those Finals when he sustained a broken neck but refused to leave the field until his team had been victorious. He took over the No.1 spot at Maine Road from another of the really great 'keepers, the late Frank Swift, former Blackpool lifeboatman. "Big Swifty" who could throw the ball from one goal to the other and was indeed a genial giant, served City for 17 years (1933-1950). He played in 341 League games, won Championship and Cup medals and 19 England caps. He became a sports journalist but lost his life in the tragic Munich air disaster of 1958 when he was returning home with the Manchester United team after a European Cup game.

It is almost impossible to give a complete list of goalies who went on and on and set up club appearance records but here are a few more: Arthur Wood with Orient

ABOVE . . . At the ripe old age of 37, Celtic's Ronnie Simpson won his first Scotland cap—against England, too.

(1921-31)—374 games; Welsh cap Tommy Farquharson of Cardiff City (1922-35)—445 games; Jim Lawrence with Newcastle United (1904-22)—432 games; John Simpson (Gillingham 1957-72)—571 games; Allan Kelly of Preston (1961-74)—447 games; Peter Bonetti who played 487 League games for Chelsea

Former pit team centre-half Sam Bartram played nearly 600 games in the Charlton goal in 22 years.

Elisha Scott, the Liverpool 'keeper, won 31 caps for Northern Ireland.

between 1960 and 1974. But the "daddy" of them all was Sam Bartram, former pit team centre-half who joined Charlton Athletic as a 'keeper in 1934 and remained at the Valley for 22 years to achieve an incredible record of 583 appearances. That is still the all-time record for a goalie with one club service. Of course there is no reason why even that remarkable total of League appearances should not be beaten in the future. It is almost certain to be bettered by one or more 'keepers whose career covers several clubs.

Gordon Banks might have done it. At the time of his tragic car crash which forced his retirement he had a total of 510 League games to his credit and could easily have become the first to reach 600. Other "veteran" 'keepers — (in service but not in age)—who could shatter all the previous records are Pat Jennings, Alex Stepney, Bill Glazier, Jim Montgomery and David Best, whose games total with Bournemouth, Oldham and Ipswich was only a few short of 500 when he joined Portsmouth in February 1974.

Like "old soldiers"—old goalies never die they only fade away, and even then they take a long time doing it. One of Liverpool's greatest players was Elisha Scott, 31 times Irish international, who was the Reds' No. 1 for 22 years. He left Anfield in 1934 to return home to continue his career with Belfast Celtic. Then what about Ronnie Simpson, son of former Rangers and Scotland centre-half Jimmy Simpson? Ron made his first appearance for Queen's Park as a schoolboy during the war, moved on to Third Lanark and then to Newcastle United to gain two FA Cup winner's medals. In 1960 he moved on to Hibs to complete his career — as we thought. But Ronnie Simpson with over 450 games behind him had other ideas. Four years later he was signed by Celtic and at the age of 37 helped the Green-and-whites to win all the Scottish trophies and the European Cup (1967). He also gained his first full Scottish cap against England—a fitting end to a fantastic career.

Just how difficult is it to become a professional footballer? What is it like for a young player to find himself lining-up with famous stars?

NO EASY ROAD

'Dedication and hard work'

BOBBY CLARK . . .
ABERDEEN

WHEN I signed for Queen's Park away back in the early Sixties it was like a dream come true. I was one of the fortunate few who made the grade and I'll always be grateful to Queen's for giving me the chance to play football.

Looking back on my early career I would say I suffered very few disappointments. There were occasional setbacks, but on the whole they were few and far between. It was just a case of lots of hard work and dedication, which is very important if you are to succeed in this game.

I remember playing in the Queen's Park team for the first time. It was a Second Division fixture at Brechin and only a few hundred fans bothered to turn up. But to me it seemed like the Cup Final. I was in the first-team and the hardest part was over.

One of the biggest thrills for a young player just starting out is to come up against a big-name performer. I remember playing against Alloa and saving a tremendous header from Willie Fernie, who had just ended his brilliant career with Celtic.

Although Queen's are an amateur club, Eddie Turnbull, who took me to Aberdeen, brought a professional outlook to Hampden during his time there. I owe him a lot for the encouragement and help he gave me in the early days. He, more than anyone, influenced my career.

Bobby fists away an Arbroath attack.

'Dropped after a few games'

THOMSON ALLAN . . .
DUNDEE

I learned very quickly that to be successful in this game you must never stop improving your basic skills. Any young player who joins a senior club must accept that there is no easy road to the top. Only those who are prepared to put their backs into the job survive at the top level.

The hardest part of all is convincing the 'boss' that you are good enough to warrant a crack at first-team football. Like most young players I was eventually given the chance to prove myself, but I soon came down to earth when I was dropped after a couple of games. That was a shattering experience.

Man in the middle . . . Dundee 'keeper Thomson Allan.

These were two of the questions SHOOT put to six Scottish First Division stars who have made good. All agree—there's . . .

TO STARDOM

My earliest triumph came when I was picked for the Scottish Youth team. It was a tremendous thrill to be involved in international football even at that level. I

have played for the full international side since then, of course, but I doubt if even appearing in front of 80,000 fans gave me quite as much of a lift.

I remember in the early days speaking to and playing against men I had admired as a youngster, stars like Bill Brown and Ronnie Simpson, and I suppose I was a bit overawed by it all. But the excitement wears-off and you come to accept these things. The thrill of playing first-team football, though, is something which never loses its edge.

'Coaching was almost unheard-of'

DOUG HOUSTON . . .
DUNDEE UNITED

I didn't encounter too many difficulties and hardships when I joined Queen's Park as a 15-year-old. Obviously you must work hard in training to build muscles and achieve fitness, but that should not be a problem to any youngster. After all, if you are not prepared to train all-out at the start of your career then you never will.

Coaching then was almost unheard-of. It was a question of getting fit and staying fit. I was never taken aside and given instructions on how the game was played, although my father did give me a lot of encouragement in the early days.

At 18 I joined Dundee, who had just won the First Division Championships, and came face to face with players I had previously hero worshipped as a schoolboy. It was a great experience to train with and play alongside men like Alan Gilzean, Ian Ure and Alex Hamilton, all of them internationals, and this benefited my career.

But the biggest thrill of all was playing against the likes of Ralph Brand, Jimmy Miller and Davie Wilson whom I had watched and followed as a youngster in Glasgow. But as you progress you begin to accept the stars as ordinary people doing a job.

On reflection I would say I was more fortunate than most because I started with a Second Division club and worked my way up. When I did join Dundee the club had enjoyed tremendous success and that made it easier. But nothing in football is easy, no matter which team you play for.

Doug Houston on the ball.

'Unwanted—in England'

JACKIE SINCLAIR . . DUNFERMLINE

It didn't take me long to realise that football is not a game for "softies". My career hadn't really begun when I found myself on the scrapheap—unwanted by Huddersfield Town, who were managed by Bill Shankly at that time.

I had joined Huddersfield on a month's trial and played a couple of games in one of the junior teams when the blow fell. Mr. Shankly told me I was too small and my career in English football came to an abrupt halt.

I went back home to Dunfermline, and thanks to Jock Stein I was saved from obscurity when he took me to East End Park.

Mr. Stein had a tremendous influence on my early career. He didn't believe in rushing young players and as a result securing a place in the first-team was a gradual process.

I had only played one full first-team game when things really started to happen for me. My moment of glory came when I made my home debut against Airdrie—and scored a hat-trick. It's the sort of thing you read about in boys' comics, but it really did happen.

I eventually moved on from Dunfermline and spent a number of years in England with Leicester City, Newcastle and Sheffield Wednesday before arriving back at East End Park two seasons ago.

I have played alongside and against players I used to idolise as a schoolboy and I have enjoyed being involved in football. But you have got to dedicate yourself to achieve success. Any youngster with the idea that it's easy might as well forget about football as a career.

Jackie Sinclair shows control.

'You must accept the knocks'

DONALD FORD . . . HEARTS

I think today's budding young professional stands a better chance of making the grade than when I started out with Hearts 11 years ago. But the same rules still apply. To be successful you must graft and be prepared to accept the knocks which are part and parcel of the game.

When I began my career at Tynecastle I was a part-time player and, therefore, had to cram more into learning what the game is all about. I didn't go into football with the idea that it would be all plain sailing, so I wasn't surprised to learn just how much I had to apply myself. Nowadays, young players get more attention and there is more specialised coaching which is a big advantage.

It was a tremendous feeling to work your way through from the junior ranks to a place in the reserve team and know that you were only one step away from achieving First Division football.

I played four or five first team

Donald Ford jumps over team-mate Drew Busby while shooting at goal.

games during the 1964-65 season, the year Hearts lost the Championship on goal average, and I will never forget the thrill I experienced when I saw my name included alongside players I had idolised as a schoolboy. Just to be present on the same field as Jim Baxter and the Scottish heroes of that time was like a dream come true.

But there are a lot of disappointments to be faced. I was a member of the Hearts team that lost the 1968 Scottish F.A. Cup Final to Dunfermline so I know what I am talking about. But it's the uncertainty about football which makes it such a great game to be involved in.

'Passed over for a first -team place'

COLIN JACKSON . . . RANGERS

When I joined Rangers it meant moving from my home in Aberdeen down to Glasgow and that's a big switch for any youngster to make. I suppose really that was the hardest part of all. I never encountered any great difficulty in training and soon came to accept all the demands.

My first real disappointment came when I was passed over for a first-team place, despite the fact that Rangers didn't really have a recognised centre-half at that time. The manager obviously thought I was a bit young for the job and Ronnie McKinnon stepped in.

Eventually I made the first-team and played a part in helping Rangers to a place in the Final of the European Cup Winners' Cup in 1967. I was only 20 at the time and got a tremendous kick out of playing a part in the club's march to the Final. Sadly, we lost out to Bayern Munich.

When I joined Rangers I found myself in the company of a host of big name players and like any youngster I was a bit owerawed by it all. But eventually I came to accept this as all part of the process of growing up in football.

It was one of these "big name" players, Jimmy Miller, who influenced my career most in the early days. He was always around to offer words of encouragement and advice and I will always be grateful for the help he gave me.

Rangers defender Colin Jackson clears his lines.

TARTAN TALK

ALLY HUNTER

'Players I admire!'

WHEN I was 15-years-old I was invited down to England to have trials with Leicester City.

Unfortunately—or thinking about it now, fortunately—I was not signed by the club, but while I was there I watched a young goalkeeper put himself through all sorts of hell during training.

He would almost knock himself out during the training sessions and then afterwards—when most of the other players had gone home—he would start hammering the ball at a corrugated fence and diving at the ball as it rebounded to it from all sorts of crazy angles.

Frankly, I was amazed by the 'keeper's enthusiasm and appetite for the game. And it paid off in the end, too . . . that youngster was Peter Shilton, now, of course, one of the greatest goalkeepers in the world. I cite Peter as one of the players I really admire.

Anyone who is prepared to work as hard as that deserves his chance. I once read an article that said Peter went through a training ritual at home that meant him hanging by his fingertips from a staircase and his mother pulling at his ankles. This exercise would strengthen his wrists, fingers, back and legs and he was said to go through this sort of exercise every night. Obviously I don't know if that particular story is completely true, but I can believe it after having seen Peter's dedication as a teenager.

What other sorts of players do I admire? There are plenty— and for many different reasons. I can admire the skills of Jimmy Johnstone and Kenny Dalglish and at the same time admire the defensive qualities of a rugged player such as Norman Hunter.

It didn't surprise me at all when Norman was named by his fellow soccer professionals as their player of the year two seasons ago. Two years ago we played the Leeds boys in the benefit match for big Jack Charlton and we won 4-3. Norman played his normal game and I didn't hear anyone say anything about his tackling. Certainly it's hard, but it's also fair and that is the main thing.

Jimmy Johnstone is a great player to play behind. He is so entertaining and he does things with the ball that other players could never even think of doing. I remember facing him when I was with Kilmarnock and we were playing Celtic in the Scottish Cup Semi-Final at Hampden. The score stood at 1-1 after the interval when suddenly wee Jimmy decided to show us what it was all about.

He started tearing holes in our left flank and he set up a chance for Dixie Deans to hammer the second goal past me and shortly after this Jimmy did it again with a mazy dribble on the right, an accurate cross and Lou Macari couldn't miss from six yards.

There were several players on view that night that I admire. One is Bobby Murdoch, who is now, of course, with Middlesbrough. Bobby was always a real gentleman on the field. He flatly refused to foul a player. That wasn't his style and he just wouldn't do it. I also admired him for his superb skills. He was so delicate at pushing the ball around, but at the same time he could bring the ball forward and finish moves with some of the most devastating shooting I have ever had to face.

Best 'Keeper

Billy McNeill is another player that must be respected. He is a Celtic player first and foremost and he is a Celtic fan, too! I can never imagine Parkhead without big Billy. His ability speaks volumes for him. His power in the air is the best in the country—no striker can look forward to playing against Billy.

John Greig may be skipper of our deadly rivals Rangers, but I still admire him. He has put so much into the game, given the lead for many youngsters to copy. He has been to Rangers what Billy McNeill has been to Celtic. He has been captain of his club and country — like Billy — and I don't think anyone would say he doesn't deserve the rewards that have gone his way.

Gordon Banks was undoubtedly the world's best goalkeeper before that unfortunate accident that ended his playing days. He was always so poised and confident. His self-assuredness must have put many strikers off even before they had touched the ball! And how many times did you see him fumble the ball? Not many, I bet.

Away from players I admire there are managers. There's Jock Stein for a start—and I'm not just saying that because he is my gaffer at Parkhead. He has done so much over the past decade that no-one could possible question his judgment. Bill Shankly, the former boss of Liverpool, was another I greatly admired.

He was a magnificent character, a stand-out personality in a game that cries out for them. It was a sad day for soccer when he quit, but he left behind so many memories to be cherished and told and retold throughout the years.

Alistair Hunter

Just three of the players Ally admires . . . Stoke 'keeper Peter Shilton (above), Middlesbrough's Bobby Murdoch (right) and team-mate Jimmy Johnstone.

Electric Shocks

LEFT . . . SACKED AFTER 44 DAYS! Controversial Brian Clough leaves Leeds after just 44 days in the "hot seat". His sacking had its compensations, though, like the reported £98,000 pay-off he received from the club.

CHESTER'S BIG NIGHT! John James (right) celebrates the goal that put Chester in the Semi-Finals of the 1974/75 League Cup at the expense of Newcastle.

BELOW . . . POLE-AXED! Poland's Grzegorz Lato (centre) turns in delight after team-mate Jan Domarski had given them the lead over England at Wembley. England fought back, but the 1-1 draw was enough to send the Poles through to the World Cup Finals.

RIGHT . . . BEST QUITS—AGAIN! The man who never seems to be out of the headlines, George Best, is in a thoughtful mood as he chats with Manchester United boss Tommy Docherty. After a couple of come-backs Bestie finally hung-up his magical United boots.

LEFT . . . FIRST AGAINST IN 19 HOURS! Following an amazing unbeaten run of 1,000-plus minutes of international football, Italy goal-keeper Dino Zoff was beaten by, of all people, Haiti's Emmanuel Sanon. In their opening World Cup Finals game, Sanon raced half the length of the field to score a goal that will never be forgotten.

BELOW . . . ENGLAND BOSS FIRED! After being the only manager to win World Cup glory with England, Sir Alf Ramsey paid the penalty of failing to qualify for the '74 Finals.

BOTTOM, LEFT . . . SUNDERLAND SINK LEEDS! One of the biggest F.A. Cup Final upsets of all time — Sunderland of Division Two beat mighty Leeds 1-0 in the 1973 Final at Wembley.

ABOVE . . . PALACE RELEGATED! Despite spending something in the region of £500,000 on new players, Crystal Palace couldn't avoid relegation to the Third Division. This picture shows Palace's last game in Division Two of 1974, when they failed to beat Cardiff and were therefore relegated.

'International'

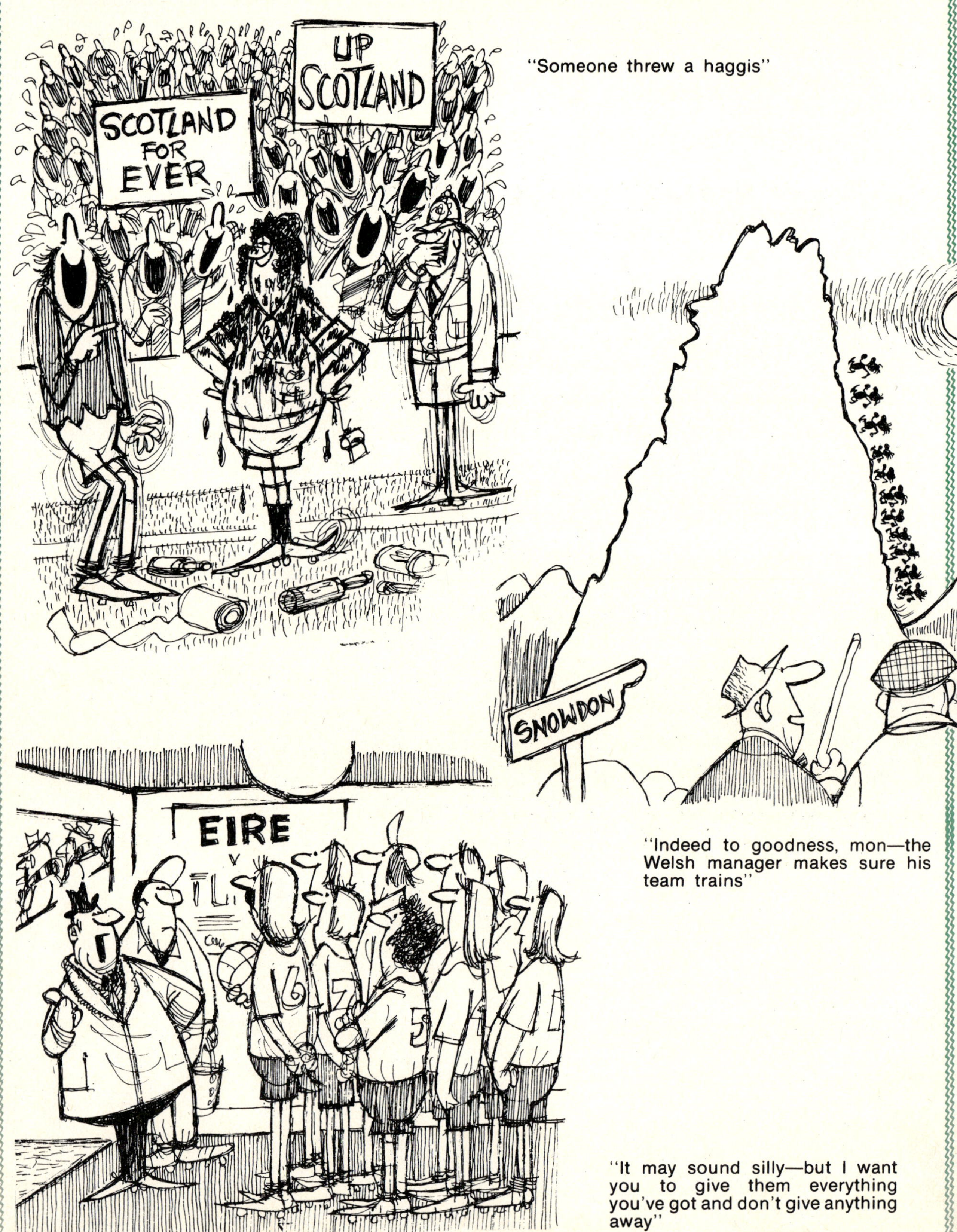

"Someone threw a haggis"

"Indeed to goodness, mon—the Welsh manager makes sure his team trains"

"It may sound silly—but I want you to give them everything you've got and don't give anything away"

Laughs

SHOOT/GOAL cartoonist STYX takes a hilarious look at soccer around the world.

"Bet that will be the last time *he'll* ref an international in Spain"

"I'm as patriotic as the next man, mate—but aren't they overdoing it?"

"But I no compre, ref. Why eez it you eez zending me off?"

"He's just made a translation of what their centre-forward called him"

The rags-to-riches star KEVIN BEATTIE

THERE is one thing certain about Ipswich Town star Kevin Beattie. He doesn't hesitate—ever. For confirmation ask the shrewd men who run Liverpool. Or ask Stoke City striker John Ritchie.

Liverpool sent for Beattie to come down from his native Carlisle for a trial. He did so. But there was no-one at the station to meet him. He kicked his heels around for a while, just a little boy lost, and then he didn't hesitate. He caught the next train home.

It was Liverpool who hesitated . . . and lost the most neon-bright star football has discovered since George Best, or Denis Law or Jimmy Greaves.

Beattie didn't hesitate when going for a 50-50 ball in a match against Stoke in October, 1974. Neither, of course, did John Ritchie. But their collision course ended with Ritchie in hospital with a bad leg break.

People blamed Beattie, including Stoke manager Tony Waddington. And others lambasted Beattie for not going to see Ritchie in hospital. Explained 20-year-old Beattie: "After all the things Ritchie and others had said about me, I didn't see much point in going along to see him in hospital."

Was Beattie to blame? A Stoke player, who obviously wishes to be anonymous, said: "I can't really blame the young fellow. He might have mistimed his tackle, but I didn't think it was reckless or deliberately 'dirty'. The kid went in to get that ball . . . and he got it."

Another certainty is that Beattie will pile up more and more honours. "He is a great player," says Ipswich boss Bobby Robson. "I mean that—a great player. He has the heart of a lion, the engine of a Rolls-Royce. He should have been in the England team when he was 19 . . . yes, even when he was 18. That's how highly I rate him."

Beattie doesn't ask for star treatment. He's one of the most modest men in the game. And he just loves his football. An hour before Ipswich met Coventry in a League exercise last season, he had a sore throat and was running a little bit of a temperature.

"I really didn't expect him to play," recalls Robson, "but he pleaded with me to give him a try-out just before the kick-off. After it, he said that he was fit to play. I doubted it, yet he went out and played a blinder as we beat the Midlands side 4-0."

After the let-down by Liverpool, it didn't take long for Ipswich to move in. They met the train, all right. And when soccer's new power boy arrived, he had only sixpence in his pocket.

"That's true—I'll swear on it," says Robson. "He had only sixpence and his trousers were rather tattered. But there was nothing tatty about the performance he turned on when we gave him a trial. We couldn't sign him quickly enough.

"Nowadays, Beattie is not short of a bob or two. His wealth should accumulate in the next few years, but he will definitely have to buy a larger cabinet for his honours."

"I like winning," explains Beattie. "That is what the game is all about. Reserve team matches, friendlies, they come alike to me. I want to win them."

He is indeed a rags to riches star. And as his reputation grows each week, Liverpool must regret the day that they missed the train.

By doing so they also missed the boat. Anyone in or around Ipswich will tell you that.

SOCCER—CONTINENTAL STYLE!

Real Madrid's West German star Gunter Netzer speaks very good English, like many Continental stars.

WHEN we no longer remember the 5th of November with a bonfire in the backyard, the fireworks manufacturers will probably move to Southern Italy: scarcely a match goes by at Naples, for example, without a cascade of firecrackers to announce their team's arrival and their every goal.

That arrival, incidentally, is by means of an underground tunnel with heavily-reinforced steel doors that can be slammed shut behind the retreating teams and officials in the event of the pitch being invaded—although that in itself would be difficult enough as the spectators are shut in behind a moat and wire netting.

All this would suggest that the Italian fan, indeed that all Latin spectators, are a very dangerous species indeed. But the closing of grounds in Spain and Italy at the first sign of trouble has drastically reduced incidents at grounds, and outside them outbreaks of violence are rare.

There is little question, for example, of Rome shopkeepers ever boarding up their windows because Milan supporters have come to town, as happens when so-called supporters of Manchester United and other British clubs descend on hitherto peaceful communites like cowhands at the end of a long cattle drive in the wild, wild West. Trouble on trains is virtually unknown, and that hackneyed old weapon, the toilet roll streamer, is rarely seen.

Roger MacDonald highlights some of the amazing differences between the way the game is played in Britain and Europe.

Possibly the British policeman's reputation for restraint encourages our hooligans, who would get short shrift from the riot police in France, Italy or Spain, where the principle is to take as few prisoners as possible. Rangers' fanatics found this to their cost when their club played against Moscow Dynamo in the European Cup-Winners' Cup Final at Barcelona: the returning plane-loads of Scots looked like an airborne version of, 'Emergency Ward Ten'.

Young offenders are also treated with comparative leniency in British courts, because imprisonment in this country is still comparatively rare. Magistrates, too, can take their time about deciding whether to charge someone arrested, as some Manchester United fans discovered in Belgium at the start of last season, when a few of their number spent weeks in jail without ever coming to court.

If anyone is at risk on the Continent, it is the poor old referee, subject to abuse by players and spectators alike, and tempted by bribes from leading clubs in important matches. All too often, in Italy especially, the referee has to be smuggled out of the stadium by some subterfuge that would have done credit to an episode of 'Colditz'. Italian players have been fined, even suspended, for voicing their criticisms of the referee. But officials' honesty can sometimes be in doubt, and stories of bribery are rife on the Continent. In Greece, for example, foreign referees are drafted in for important matches because the integrity of local officials is so much in doubt.

As in Britain, referees are generally not well-paid in comparison with the players, which makes a few of them open to influence by wealthy Continental clubs. In European Cup-ties, for example, some teams have taken advantage of the custom of giving officials a memento of their visit, by

BELOW . . . Ugly scenes after the Rangers/Moscow Dynamo Cup-Winners' Cup Final. Fans and Spanish police clashed in Barcelona.
RIGHT . . . Ferenc Puskas, the great Hungarian forward, was an Army Major who attended parade for half an hour each month!

SOCCER–CONTINENTAL STYLE! *continued*

providing lavish gifts of watches and jewellery, carefully placed in their dressing-room *before* the game.

Some Continental players, of course, earn far more than their British counterparts, with salaries for Italian internationals reputed to be in excess of £30,000 a year. But their real rewards come from signing-on fees which, unlike here, are not limited to ten per cent of their transfer fee or subject to the move coming at the club's request. Johan Cruyff, for instance, received £460,000 for moving from Ajax Amsterdam to Barcelona and several other players have had sums in excess of £50,000.

But the *average* salary of the Continental footballer is about the same as in Britain, especially outside the leading clubs. West Germany and France, for instance, have only one national Division, and players in the lower, regional Leagues, are part-time professionals who need another job outside the game to earn a living. In Eastern Europe, of course, sometimes these jobs are purely nominal, enabling countries such as Hungary and East Germany to preserve the fiction that their players are amateurs. Hungary's most famous player, Ferenc Puskas, was an army major who attended parade for half an hour once a month!

As all the signs are that many of Britain's 120-odd League teams will soon be compelled to employ more and more part-time professionals, or even amateurs, and that the Divisions could eventually be re-organised on a regional basis, how do some of our richer neighbours make football ends meet? The answer is that many draw their funds from big companies, among them Juventus, controlled by the Agnelli family of the Fiat motor company, and PSV Eindhoven, subsidised by the big Dutch electrical firm, Philips.

Intense Rivalry

Others such as Barcelona and Naples, rely heavily on a huge income from season ticket holders, more than 80,000 at Barcelona and over 60,000 in Naples. Many Eastern European clubs are financed out of military funds, such as Red Army Moscow, Honved Budapest, Dukla Prague, and Red Star Belgrade. While in France, many clubs are kept going by funds from the local council—imagine your fathers' reaction if they were told that Chelsea needed a centre-forward, so that would mean an extra fiver on the rates!

Continental clubs often make better use of their stadium than British sides, whose grounds are invariably left empty for as much as a fortnight at a time. Abroad, clubs are multi-sport organisations, such as Real Madrid, who have a huge family membership at their sports complex, and are almost as famous in Europe for their basketball as they are for their football.

But rivalries are just as intense on the Continent, and very few major clubs in Western Europe are prepared to share a ground with their neighbours. Atletico Madrid, for instance, found the money for a new stadium, Manzanares, to replace their aging Estadio Metropolitano, rather than go in with Real; Lisbon's principal teams, Sporting and Benfica, recently abandoned a plan to use one ground because the clubs could not agree on whose should be sold. One of the few exceptions is

LEFT . . . Lazio versus Inter-Milan. Before Italian League games, the players go away to a training-camp. After the match, the poor referee often has to be smuggled out of the ground in a disguise.

BELOW . . . Borussia Monchengladbach versus Fortuna Dusseldorf in West Germany's only national League, the Bundesliga.

the San Siro stadium, shared by AC Milan and Inter-Milan, but that is owned by the municipality—an advantage also enjoyed by Bayern Munich, who use the superb stadium built for the 1972 Olympics.

While football in Britain is largely subsidised, almost patronised, by the self-made director who has worked for his money rather than inherited it, on the Continent it also attracts politicians, professional men and the landowning classes. Even General de Gaulle, who is supposed to have detested football, felt compelled from time to time to attend the French Cup Final, while many an Italian First Division club has a member of the old nobility somewhere among its directors. The players, too, enjoy a dignified role in society that makes them welcome at almost any important function, and not simply in the season when they have won the league or the cup.

As in Britain, promising players become the target of the big clubs almost as soon as they leave the cradle. The leading Italian sides, Inter-Milan, AC Milan and Juventus have spent vast sums on youth schemes, and AC Milan's facilities for young players at Milanello consist of almost a small town devoted to teaching footballers.

And not just football either: have you noticed how many Continental players speak excellent English and other foreign languages, while our players, like the rest of our population, are usually struggling in pigeon French? Two of Germany's best players, Gunter Netzer and Paul Breitner, can hold their own in English and Spanish; while Johan Cruyff held a remarkable press conference during the last World Cup simultaneously in four languages, switching from one to the other like a United Nations' interpreter.

Locked Away

Only the Germans, East and West, consistently play their League matches on a Saturday, although some countries, France and Portugal among them, sometimes spread their programme over the whole weekend to allow fans to see more than one game if they wish. That must come in Britain, although I doubt whether we will ever quite see the full theatrical display of the Sunday Continental Match.

The players are locked away from wives and girlfriends for two or three days before the game—at Barcelona the club even has its own private chapel so no-one can escape by asking to go to Mass. Many families organise themselves to go to church at midday, where as often as not they will hear a prayer for their club's success; and the stadium at four, when the sun has lost its intensity. Father will sound the horn of his battered old saloon just as madly as the rest in the inevitable traffic jam, then abandon the car if necessary in the middle of the road rather than risk missing a few minutes' play.

Fortunately the match rarely starts on time, delayed by endless announcements and a posse of photographers; it ends still farther behind schedule, after a long half-time interval and countless stoppages for injury that bring more white-coated attendants on to the field than are needed for a heart surgery. The final whistle sparks off a rat-tat-tat of firecrackers and the bedlam switches to the dressing-rooms, which are open house for the press, notables and hangers-on alike. The winning manager expects, and receives, applause; basking in the reflected glory of his team's success even if he has only been in charge for a week. After all, to be a hero, as Wellington might have observed after Waterloo, one only needs to be there when it happens.

'I don't miss London'

Alan Hudson, Stoke

FOR someone who is still nearer 20 than 30, Alan Hudson has a lot of soccer memories.

He can look back on a meteoric rise to fame that had England manager Don Revie saying: "There is no limit to what this boy can achieve."

Then came the agony of missing the 1970 F.A. Cup Final—with Chelsea, of course—when he had to watch his team-mates overcome Leeds to land the Cup.

A year later Alan's career looked rosy as he inspired Chelsea to a European Cup-Winners' Cup victory over the famous Real Madrid.

In 1972 Alan finally made it to Wembley, but Chelsea were beaten 2-1 in the League Cup Final . . . by Stoke City, of all clubs.

In 1974, Alan's career turned a complete circle when he left the club he had been with all his career for their League Cup conquerors, Stoke.

The transfer was not a particularly pleasant one and many unpleasant things were said in the heat of the moment.

Alan was worried about his form . . . Chelsea about their slide from the top . . . and the result was a none-too-nice atmosphere as Alan moved north.

It was a transfer that surprised many people, who expected Londoner Alan to stay in the capital.

He has no regrets about his complete change of environment — not now anyway.

Alan recalls: "When I arrived in Stoke, it was pouring with rain and blowing a gale. Not exactly picture-postcard stuff.

"Then I came to my senses and realised I was there to play football, not look at the scenery."

The move was a challenge because Alan's form immediately before the transfer was, as he puts it, "pretty rubbishy."

"The boss — Tony Waddington — said a lot of favourable things about me and I was determined not to let him down.

"I admit that I did some silly things in London. I let matters get on top of me and didn't have the right attitude to the game.

"I still had confidence in my own ability, though, and was determined to knuckle down and show I could play."

Waddington gave Alan a roving midfield role, which suited him far more than the more restricted "wide on the right" position he had been operating in at Chelsea.

Stoke rose from near the bottom to near the top of the First Division.

The Big City Boy had come good away from the bright lights and trendy night clubs.

"Leaving London was the best move I ever made," Alan says honestly.

"I've got a fabulous house in the countryside and I don't miss the capital at all.

"My family travel up regularly so everything is just right."

Stoke supporters will echo that sentiment!

Alan comes away with the ball, despite a slide-tackle by Leeds' Trevor Cherry.

You've never had it so good, Ref!

SO the ref has it rough? What with barracking crowds, press and telly inquests, argumentative players. But has he ever had to change for a game in a cow-shed? Has he ever been tossed in a river for stopping a match? Has he ever been described in the press as a 'nincompoop'? No, of course not. So let him spare a thought for his colleagues who have—in the bad old days when the ref was considered more of a nuisance than a necessity.

Who needed referees? Not the gentlemen players—a sense of fair-play was all they required. And certainly not the FA; it managed quite nicely for more than ten years without any match supervision at all. So how did the ref first get in on the act?

If gentlemen players could rely on their honour, Derbyshire yokels apparently couldn't. Fisticuffs were more in their line when it came to disputes. So when a match got out of hand, they appealed to "a disinterested spectator" to give an impartial decision. What odds on finding one from the Kop?

This example was soon followed up—by the Sheffield Association in the 1870s, and at the Public schools, Harrow and Eton.

At the latter, the ref had a particularly formidable task.

As boys will be boys, the players would often ignore simply spoken commands. So the ref was directed: 'If one of them falls on the ball, or crawls with it between his legs, if possible force him to rise.'

Modern referees may not be well paid, but in our grandfathers' day, they were lucky to receive any payment at all. What's more, they were condemned to appalling conditions of work It wasn't unusual for the ref to be asked to get changed in a barn or a cowshed. And sometimes, he changed with the players, where the atmosphere was scarcely more pleasant.

Refereeing could also be dangerous. Today, the referee is protected from angry spectators—the police see to that. But in times past, he risked the violence of an angry crowd at every match. One referee, who stopped a Derbyshire match, incurred the wrath of a number of factory girls, who stripped him naked and threw him into the river Derwent.

Whatever the attitude of public and players, the press of today is firm in its support of the ref. Times have certainly changed.

"Of all the nincompoops," one

Edwardian journalist wrote, "that ever appeared on the turf in the guise of referee, the one who attempted the job on Saturday was the worst we have ever seen!" Just imagine Jimmy Hill saying that on 'Match of the Day'.

Not even the law took the referee's side. One ref, called to give evidence in court, described his occupation, and was told by the magistrate: "Refereeing is not an occupation, sir, it's a disease." Believe us ref, you've never had it so good!

Incidents and quotations from:
Association Football & The Men Who Made it.
By Alfred Gibson & William Pickford.
Published by The Caxton Publishing Company (1906).

Gerd the Goal

Gerd was the top scorer in the 1970 World Cup Finals. Here's one (left) against Peru—while below, Der Bomber heads one home against Kickers Offenbach.

Congratulations! Gerd celebrates a goal against Borussia Monchengladbach.

From his favourite close-in position, Gerd scores against 1.FC Kaiserslautern.

Germany's third against Russia in the 1968 European Championship Final.

THERE can be no doubt that Europe's most prolific goalscorer in recent years is Gerd Muller, ace striker of Bayern Munich and West Germany. His goals have helped to win the European Championship, World Cup and European Cup. . . not forgetting his many goals on the German domestic scene. Here, we take a closer look at just a few of the hundreds of goals scored by this extremely accurate marksman.

The 1974 European Cup Final against Atletico Madrid . . . Bayern won 4-0 in a replay. Here's goal number two.

BELOW . . . Down, but not out. Gerd on the mark against Yugoslavia in the 1974 World Cup Finals.
RIGHT . . . A quick flick against Australia—and it's a goal.

The goal that won the World Cup for West Germany. Holland leave Gerd unmarked for a second—and they pay the penalty as Der Bomber makes it 2-1 . . . which is how the 1974 World Cup Final ended.

Soccer stars of

ACCORDING to the astrologists, our lives and careers are determined by the stars. The different signs of the Zodiac possess their own characteristics which forge our personalities and hold the key to our fate.

Of course not everyone conforms to these categories. But let's take a look at some of our top soccer stars to see how they fit into the pattern.

ALAN BALL (Arsenal)

You could not find anyone more typical of *ARIES* than Liverpool defender Tommy Smith (Born April 5). The Aries person is very much a firebrand or battering-ram. He will forge his way through life with courage, energy, initiative and an aggressive instinct. He is a true pioneer.

What better description of "Tommy the Tank", who captained Liverpool in the gloriously successful Shankly era?

Incidentally Brian Clough comes under the sign of Aries

The *TAURUS* characteristics of patience and perseverance are seen clearly in Arsenal and England midfield dynamo Alan Ball (Born May 5).

Alan looked a likely England captain before England's summer tour of 1974. But a broken leg in Arsenal's last match of the 1973-74 season put him out of the running. Further disappointment awaited him. On his comeback he broke an ankle.

That would have been enough to discourage a lot of men. But Alan fought back to fitness and was soon in the England side again — and as captain.

PAT JENNINGS (Spurs)

It is said that if the intelligent, versatile *GEMINI* character had an animal symbol, it would be a monkey. One of the Gemini types in the football world is 'Spurs and Northern Ireland keeper Pat Jennings (Born June 12).

Pat's agility is often reminiscent of the jungle (though in the nicest possible way) as he leaps from post to post to keep out certain goals.

JOHN HOLLINS (Chelsea)

John Hollins (Born July 16) has plenty of the team-spirit and devotion to the cause which is characteristic of those born under the sign of *CANCER*.

Throughout Chelsea's problems he remained a model teamman and always put the interests of his club before anything else.

Cancer types are generally sympathetic and protective and here again John fits the bill. His captaincy was notable for the way in which he nursed Chelsea's youngsters through their early games.

Another Chelsea star Ian Hutchinson (Born August 4) is the exact prototype of the *LEONIAN.*

Dignified, powerful and brave as a lion, Ian has earned a reputation for having one of the biggest

Emlyn Hughes

Ian Hutchinson

hearts in football. Two broken legs and countless minor injuries have done nothing to dent Ian's enthusiasm for soccer. He is still to be seen going in fearlessly where the action is toughest.

Emlyn Hughes (August 28) was born under the sign of *VIRGO*, but in many ways he is the direct opposite to the typical Virgoan. They are usually more suited to being the power behind the throne rather than on the throne itself.

This could hardly be said of the Liverpool and England captain whose drive and enthusiasm have proved admirably suited to the demands of leadership.

Virgoans tend to be detached and reserved. But Emlyn shows no shortage of involvement as he gets stuck into the game.

Those born under *LIBRA* are artists rather than grafters. They strive for harmony and beauty. They are calm and happy. Therefore it comes as no surprise to learn that one of the best known footballing Librans is Charlie Cooke (born

Charlie Cooke

October 14,) the Chelsea inside-forward, who is a true craftsman in the art of ball control. Charlie's midfield skills make Chelsea tick and his dribbling wizardry is very much due to his superb balance.

Mike Channon (Born November 11) has a deep love for the countryside. He has led a "double life" for many years, combining football with the down-to-earth business of farming. Mike is a keen horseman and is owner of a racehorse. Mike is a quiet person off the field and the passionate devotion to things which mean a

Mike Channon

lot to him make him a worthy example of the *SCORPIO* breed. He showed with Southampton in both Divisions One and Two that he is a consistent goalscorer.

A degree in politics and economics at Warwick University by Steve Heighway (Born November 25)

Soccer stars of the Zodiac continued

make him a more than suitable representative of the *SAGITTARIANS*. This sign is noted

STEVE HEIGHWAY (Liverpool)

for its intellectual qualities and those born under it are generally lovers of freedom and wide open spaces.

Watching Steve burst down the touch-line to give a full-back the slip, it's easy to judge to which sign he belongs.

MALCOLM MACDONALD (Newcastle)

CAPRICORN is the Zodiac sign of Malcolm Macdonald (Born January 7), who often receives the adulation of the Geordies for his goal scoring feats.

Newcastle and England striker 'Supermac' shows the sure-footedness of the Capricornian goat as he accepts gilt-edged goal chances from all angles. Ambition, strength of character and a clear, precise mind are other Capricornian characteristics shared by Malcolm.

AQUARIANS have the reputation for being original, independent personalities—Eusebio (Born January 25) for example. No one can deny the original individual flair of that World Cup star of 1966 and outstanding personality in the Portugal team.

And it is not suprising that the

EUSEBIO (Benfica)

fabulous Sir Stanley Matthews (Born February 1) is also an Aquarian as indeed is Danny Blanchflower (Born February 10) and Kevin Keegan (Born February 14).

Although Colin Bell (Born February 26) has been in the limelight for many years, he has always remained something of a mystery. It's as though his personality is shrouded behind a veil.

The reason for this is simple. Colin is just a typical *PISCEAN* who prefers to remain in the background and doesn't seek headlines.

Pisceans give selfless service as has Colin to England and Manchester City and many have a gift for clairvoyancy. Opponents have often considered Colin to possess psychic powers after a moment of his genius has transformed a match.

COLIN BELL (Man. City)

From these brief studies, it is apparent that an uncannily accurate picture of a player's character can be obtained from the stars.

Who knows The time might come when managers, planning tactics for forthcoming matches, will turn to astrological charts to gain inside information on opposing teams!

Keith Eddy
Sheffield United

Eddie Colquhoun
Sheffield United

STING-RAY

A closer look at some of the super saves of one of the world's top goalkeepers . . . Liverpool's Ray Clemence. Ray's career began in the lower regions of the League with Scunthorpe. Upon joining Liverpool, he "served his time" in the reserves, taking in the atmosphere of a big-time club. Now, Ray is recognised as one of the top goalies in the world, with a string of England caps to his credit.

The main picture on this page shows Ray timing his leap perfectly to collect a tricky centre. Below, Ray uses his body to full effect to shield the ball from an onrushing striker.

ABOVE
That's mine! An acrobatic jump saves the day once again for Liverpool. It's this sort of save that makes Ray not only one of the most effective, but also one of the most thrilling 'keepers in England.

RIGHT
At full stretch, Ray manages to tip this shot round the post for a corner.

BELOW
Under pressure, Ray uses his fist to clear the danger against Manchester City.

'I WANTED TO PLAY FOR BRENTFORD'

says Q.P.R. star Gerry Francis

NEXT year should signal the most important period in the career of Gerry Francis. The 23-year-old Queens Park Rangers captain and England midfield star is being strongly tipped for the captaincy in the next World Cup—providing England qualify!

Yet Francis is one of a rare breed—one who became a footballer quite by accident.

True, Gerry captained the Acton, Brentford and Chiswick junior district team, and won a few honours in the process. But when he moved on to secondary school he found no competitive soccer, only rugby. So the young Francis began to despair of following in his father's footsteps—Roy, his dad was a professional with Brentford—and settled instead for an England schoolboy trial as an outside half.

That's when the accidents started to happen. Says Gerry: "I didn't make it at rugby for England, but I wasn't all that worried because I had always wanted to be a footballer. But when you aren't playing for your district side you don't get easily noticed. Then a friend asked me to turn out on Sundays for a Chiswick soccer team. I was 15 and I was playing with men a lot older than myself. Queens Park Rangers got to hear about it, and Derek Healy, who was their chief scout, invited me down to Shepherds Bush for trials.

"I didn't really want to go. I wanted to join Brentford, where my Dad played, and where I had always enjoyed going. It looked as if it might work out that way, for Rangers said they didn't think I would make it.

"But they saw me play a couple of times, changed their minds and invited me to sign schoolboy forms.

"The rest followed. I played in the South East Counties League youth team, joined the club as an apprentice, made my debut as a substitute against Liverpool when I was 16 and my first full debut at Portsmouth the following year as a 17-year-old.

"We won 3-1 that day and I was lucky enough to score one of the goals.

"In those early days I played everywhere. I was a centre-forward, a right-winger, and it wasn't until Gordon Jago came to Rangers that I moved back to midfield, the position I like best."

It is not surprising Francis enjoys his midfield spot. He had the patience to work at his game and wait for the honours. They came at the end of the season before last when Sir Alf Ramsey picked him for the England Under-23 team against Denmark as one of the former England boss's final acts.

A few months later Francis was chosen for the full England squad by new manager Don Revie, and made his debut against Czechoslovakia.

Says Gerry: "I'll always remember that game. I felt the flu coming on and I spent so long worrying about whether I should play, and whether the cold would hold out that I didn't have time to feel the tension of my first cap at Wembley. But as soon as I heard I had been chosen I went out and sent telegrams to all the people who had helped me.

"People tend to forget this part of their careers, that there are many people who have helped them put it all together. They reach the top and sometimes believe they have done it all themselves. They haven't, you know. The best help to me? There have been so many — my Dad, Gordon Jago, Bobby Campbell, Steve Burtenshaw, and going back to the days of Alec Stock and Bill Dodgin and the apprentice team trainer. I owe them all so much."

TREVOR LOSES THAT 'SUPERBOY' TAG

TREVOR FRANCIS, Birmingham City's brilliant striker, celebrated his 21st birthday last season (April 19th, 1975) and was at last able to rid himself of the nickname "superboy," which he attained when he burst on to the soccer scene as a 16-year-old apprentice player for Blues and scored 15 goals in as many matches.

Francis has now settled down to being a very mature player and his future, both with Blues and on the International scene for England, looks very bright.

"I've now had six years in professional soccer," says Francis, "and I still have a great appetite for the game. In fact, I would say that since my marriage in July, 1974, I have been playing the best soccer of my career."

Francis met his wife, Helen on holiday in Majorca, and his debut season as a married man heralded a new-look Francis with revitalized goal scoring abilities, but on the eve of his debut for England he sustained a serious injury.

"That injury couldn't have come at a worse time," recalls Trevor, "I was top goal-scorer in Division One and Don Revie had chosen me for his very first England squad. We were playing at Sheffied United four days before the England match and I ruptured a tendon in my left-leg."

The injury kept Francis out of first-team soccer for several months, but he is now making up for lost time.

"Injuries are an occupational hazard," he says, "but I learned a lot from sitting on the sidelines. I now want to develop my game and become a utility player — operating from midfield but capable of popping up anywhere and everywhere.

"My favourite role is as a striker and I love scoring goals, but I have discovered that there is more to the game than the glories of goal-scoring. I like to think of myself as a creative player and can gain just as much satisfaction from making an opening for one of my fellow forwards.

"Though I've never been consciously selfish in my approach to the game, I am now more keyed up to team football. Blues play as a unit and I believe we are one of the most attack-minded teams in soccer at the present time.

"This is why we always get good gates at St. Andrews. Football should be more than a game involving 22 men. It should also be an entertainment. Negative football that produces goal-less draws doesn't attract crowds."

Francis is the type of player who shudders at the prospect of no goals in a League match. Birmingham City have been involved in such matches, but it doesn't often happen.

He himself is a veritable goal-scoring machine. As a schoolboy he scored hundreds of goals for school teams, and was in fact playing for Plymouth Schools when spotted by Blues chief scout, Don Dorman.

That was when Francis was 15, and one year later he was playing with the first-team and setting the soccer scene alight with his abilities.

All this happened six years ago, but that "superboy" tag remained with him until last season. Now he is known as plain Trevor Francis—a name which looks destined to earn its owner a place among the all-time greats.

THE BEST OF '74

We pick a team from the top stars of the 1974 World Cup Finals

	TOMASZEWSKI	
VOGTS	**LUIS PEREIRA** **BECKENBAUER**	**F. MARINHO**
NEESKENS	**DEYNA**	**VAN HANEGEM**
LATO	**MULLER**	**CRUYFF**

GOALKEEPER
Jan Tomaszewski (Poland)

AFTER doing more than anybody to ensure Poland and not England went to West Germany, Jan (pronounced Yan) proved once and for all that he is a goalkeeper of unorthodox world-class.

He may not have the grace of Banks or the style of Zoff, but in his own way Jan is every bit as good.

Tomaszewski brilliantly saves a penalty by Sweden's Steffan Tapper.

In the Finals, he brilliantly saved two penalties and countless other "certainties".

Big and brave, he is not afraid to come off his line and looking back at his performances in Germany, it is difficult to fault the man once labelled "a clown" by a certain English manager.

RIGHT-BACK
Berti Vogts (West Germany)

HIS blot-out of Holland's Johan Cruyff in the actual Final earned little Berti his place in our team, although throughout the tournament he had been outstanding.

Berti has mastered the art of man-to-man marking, the defensive system favoured by the Germans, and sticks to his man like a limpet.

Sound in defence, Berti breaks forward at every opportunity and his speed off the mark make him an extremely difficult opponent in every department.

Still the right side of 30, Berti will surely, bar injuries, be around in 1978 to help Germany defend the title.

STOPPER
Luis Pereira (Brazil)

ALTHOUGH Pereira operated more as a sweeper in the Finals, his physical power and heading ability enable him to fill both roles with equal effectiveness.

A mean customer, Pereira typified the "they shall not pass" tactics of Brazil '74, although in fairness it must be said that he did his job superbly.

He blotted his copybook by being sent-off (rightly) against Holland, but Pereira had already done enough to make us all realise that Brazil can produce world-class defenders as well as strikers.

ABOVE . . . West Germany's Berti Vogts.

LEFT . . . Brazil's Luis Pereira.

SWEEPER
Franz Beckenbauer (West Germany)

AFTER finishing second in 1966 and third in 1970, Franz finally collected his long-overdue World Cup winners' medal in front of his own fans.

Undoubtedly one of the all-time "greats", Franz was the pioneer of the attacking sweeper, coming forward from his defensive position with deadly effect.

Franz started his career as a midfield man and it wasn't until after 1970 that he "moved back".

Some say he is wasted in defence, but he attacks so often and so well that sweeper is surely the role best suited to this incredibly talented star.

LEFT-BACK
Francisco Marinho (Brazil)

ANOTHER Brazilian defender, but with far more style and eye-catching close-control than his fellow back-four men.

Krol (Holland) and Breitner (West Germany) could lay claims

ABOVE . . . Francisco Marinho, the blond Brazilian full-back.
LEFT . . . "The Emperor"—Franz Beckenbauer of West Germany.

to this position, but Francisco's contribution to the generally disappointing Brazil side gave him the edge.

He refused to indulge in any body-checking or other dubious tactics.

Instead, he defended with the grit of a European and attacked with all the skill expected from a Brazilian.

Francisco's blond hair made him stand out on the field . . . his super-skills also put him head and shoulders above his team-mates.

MIDFIELD
Johan Neeskens (Holland)

AMAZINGLY, Johan was only 21 when he picked up his losers' medal. Arguably the most widely-talented player in the world, able to do any outfield job—including penalty-taking!

Who will ever forget the way Johan refused to be intimidated by Brazil and went on to score a beauty of a goal?

Or the way he thrilled us with his well-timed runs from midfield into the penalty-area to shoot for goal?

If any single player typifies modern football, it's Johan Neeskens.

MIDFIELD
Kazimierz Deyna (Poland)

LIKE many of his team-mates, Kazi was a revelation in the Finals, showing the elimination of England was not "just one of those things".

He was Poland's conductor in midfield, directing play with passes of almost unbelievable accuracy.

Kazi's temperament was perfect and he set an example for all to follow in every respect.

In Germany, the Poland skipper was one of the most graceful players on view, able to do just about anything he liked with the ball.

ABOVE . . . Kazimierz Deyna, the Poland captain who had a superb World Cup in 1974.
BELOW . . . Holland's Johan Neeskens (black shorts) almost scores.

THE BEST OF '74 continued

MIDFIELD
Wim van Hanegem (Holland)

THE Feyenoord star may be all left foot—what a foot, though! He was a vital player in the Holland team, with his vision and ability to pass accurately over long distances.

LEFT. . . Holland's Wim van Hanegem, shows his deadly left peg against Sweden.

The only question mark over Wim was his temperament; occasionally, he allowed referees' decisions to bother him.

From a playing point of view he was superb, strong in defence adding a wide range of skills to the exciting Holland team.

STRIKER
Grzegorz Lato (Poland)

THE "find" of the Finals, Grzegorz was the top scorer with nine goals.

His speed, balance and, above all, finishing, made him a deadly opponent and he had the sort of style that made it likely he'd score with every chance!

For a small player, Grzegorz is good in the air—he managed a couple of goals with his head.

But it was when he raced towards goal that he was at his best which, in the end, proved to be better than any other forward in the world.

STRIKER
Johan Cruyff (Holland)

VOTED The Most Exciting Player of the World Cup Finals by SHOOT/GOAL readers, Johan proved that what he could do at club level, he could also do in the international team.

It is difficult, no, impossible, to list all Johan's attributes in a few paragraphs.

ABOVE . . . Gerd Muller is grounded, but still manages to score against Yugoslavia.

Of all his many techniques, perhaps his speed is the most valuable . . . the way he can leave defenders tackling his shadow after a burst of breathtaking speed.

Pele didn't play in Germany, but it is fair to call Johan his successor as the World's Most Exciting Star—just as our readers did.

STRIKER
Gerd Muller (West Germany)

ALMOST inevitably, it was "Der Bomber" who won the World Cup for West Germany with a characteristic goal from close range.

Top scorer in 1970, Gerd's goal account was not quite as full in '74, but he reaffirmed that he is a striker of the highest class.

No player is more dangerous around the six-yard box. Gerd calls them his "little goals" . . . an ironic description considering the big games they've won!

Gerd is undoubtedly the world's top striker over the past six years.

With him in their side, Germany were always likely to score at least once.

RIGHT . . . The one and only Johan Cruyff.
BELOW . . . Grzegorz Lato of Poland, top scorer of the '74 Finals.

SUBSTITUTES

RONNIE HELLSTROM . . . the courageous Sweden goalkeeper
JIM HOLTON . . . so dominant for Scotland
BILLY BREMNER . . . who led Scotland with bravery and determination
RAINER BONHOF . . . the much-under-rated West German midfielder
ROBERT GADOCHA . . . Poland's left-winger flyer

MIKE DOYLE

Manchester City's Mr. 100 per cent

MANCHESTER CITY have rightly won a reputation over the years for playing open, attacking football.

Despite changes in the team, their forward line has always had plenty of goal-power . . . some might say "just as well because their defence is suspect".

Well, it's said that the best form of defence is attack, but that doesn't really give credit to Mike Doyle, a player of vast experience and no little skill.

He's alternated between a role in the back-four and that of midfield ball-winner and it is a shame that his contribution is often overshadowed by his goalscoring team-mates.

Does he mind? "Not really. I enjoy playing and as long as the manager thinks I'm doing a good job, that's the main thing.

"I know my duties are mainly defensive, but I like to go up and have a pop at goal when I can. Over the years I've managed one or two goals that have made our forwards jealous."

It is amazing that at one time City were willing to let Mike go and it only needed his okay to become a Stoke player, by all accounts.

"I have never wanted to leave Maine Road", Mike confesses. "I supported City as a boy, and for me they're the only club I want to play for".

Fair Play

It is this professional, no-nonsense approach that makes Mike one of the game's great competitors.

While he never gives less than 100 per cent, he denies that he is a rough player.

"No matter how good a striker is, he can still be marked out of the game by fair means and this has been my attitude throughout my career.

"Things can happen in the heat of the moment, granted, but we at City have never had a 'chopper' in the true sense of the word.

"Over the past couple of years I have noticed a big improvement in discipline on the field.

"Defenders think twice about bringing down forwards where previously even the threat of a booking wouldn't have deterred them.

"Last season Rodney Marsh and Dennis Tueart were magic. Rodney has been a big name for years, but Dennis surprised me.

"I didn't realise he had so much ability and the good thing was that both players were allowed to express themselves.

"Generally speaking, 1974/75 was one of the cleanest seasons I can remember and I think credit here must go to the players more than anybody.

"Fans love to see skilful players in full flight and there was a period when they simply weren't allowed to get on with their game.

"This, for me changed last season and it can only benefit everybody concerned with football".

Wise words . . . and City, perhaps more than anyone, benefited from the change of attitude.

After a few seasons away from the honours, 1974/75 saw them back to their best.

Maybe their defence is overshadowed by their forwards. But don't underestimate the contribution of Mike Doyle . . . City's Mr. 100 per cent.

City's Dennis Tueart (centre) in full flight against Arsenal.

DAVID STRINGER
Norwich City

'HOTSHOT' COOLS OFF

LEEDS and Scotland striker Peter Lorimer is reckoned to have just about the hottest shot in the League. His thunderbolts have thrilled the fans and given opposing goalkeepers many nervous moments. Here, Hotshot cools off preparing for another thundering game!

"Just call me 'Globe-trotter Greig'"

TARTAN TALK

JOHN GREIG

HAVE boots will travel .... that could be my motto after the wonderful tours I have been on with my club Rangers and my country.

Every time I look at a globe I have to pinch myself to make sure I really have been in all the places that spin in front of me. I've almost lost count of the number of countries I have visited.

Sweden, Austria, Russia, Portugal, Denmark, Yugoslavia, West and East Germany, Holland, Bulgaria, Poland, Spain, Belgium, Norway, Italy and Turkey to name but a few!

Obviously there have been many unforgettable moments on my travels, some sad and some happy. I'll never forget the joy I felt in Barcelona when Rangers won the European Cup-winners' Cup after beating Moscow Dynamo 3-2. Nor will I ever forget the sadness I felt when we went down in the Final of the same tournament to Bayern Munich in West Germany after a late goal in extra-time.

Which countries do I prefer? I must admit I like West Germany. I have played there about eight times I think and the most enjoyable thing is that there are no drastic changes to what we are used to at home. For

John and Bayern Munich skipper Werner Olk shake hands before the 1967 Cup Winners' Cup Final in Nuremburg.

A bearded John Greig in action against Moscow Dynamo in 1972.

instance, the food is much the same. So is the climate and the football pitches. That cannot be said for every country I have visited, believe me.

I've seen some pitches that haven't had a blade of grass and been in such bad condition you would have been forgiven for thinking a herd of elephants had just charged across them. We played Ancaragucu of Turkey a couple of seasons ago and the first leg was away from home. I could hardly believe my eyes when we were taken to see the pitch. I thought it was all a dreadful joke. Unfortunately, it wasn't.

The pitch hadn't seen water in years by the look of it. There was sand everywhere and I couldn't help wondering what it was all about. Here we were to play a vitally important European match and we were going to play on a surface that school kids back home wouldn't even use. However, I'm happy to say all went well in the end and we won away from home and at Ibrox. Now every time we are in a European draw I keep my fingers crossed we miss Turkey!

But let's get back to Germany. I have a lot of respect for the way they play and their organisation on and off the field. The fans there are intelligent enough to applaud good football from the other side and you know if you win or get a draw you won't be stoned as you leave the stadium afterwards.

Holland is just like Germany. You can get steaks and salads there just like back home and again the pitches are in good condition and you are made welcome by the opposing players and the fans. You'll get a tough, hard game, of course, but never anything outside the laws of the game.

The countries I don't like visiting—apart from Turkey—are Latin countries. You can come across a lot of difficulties on these trips. For a start no-one at Ibrox would think of eating the local food. We pack up with a huge hamper when we leave Ibrox with the sort of grub we are used to and we take our own chef.

Again in some countries you encounter teams trying to put one over on you before the game. I'm certain any player who has ever played in Europe will know what I am talking about.

Sometimes they refuse to show you the pitch on which you will play, other times they refuse to give you training facilities. And another thing some do is to give you magnificent training facilities—and NO balls to play with! It has happened several times to us, I assure you.

I'm glad to say that when teams come to Ibrox no-one makes things difficult for them. They are given a tour of the ground, given all the facilities they would need and, if need be, we always try to book them into an hotel that is close enough to the stadium yet far away from the hustle and bustle of Glasgow to make sure they settle in okay.

I couldn't possibly end this article without a word about the amazing fans Rangers have dotted throughout the world. No matter where we go we have fans there. I've played in America and Canada and we have a lot of fans there with their own supporters' clubs and they always seem to be so well informed with everything that is going on. I even played in Israel in a Challenge Match and we had fans there, too. Astonishing, isn't it?

Yes, it's no wonder I pinch myself when recalling the wonderful memories soccer has provided me with and all the countries I have visited. Just call me Globe-trotter Greig.

John Greig

PAT HOWARD
Newcastle Utd.

JOHN RICHARDS
Wolves

YOU'RE just twelve yards out from goal, and only the 'keeper stands between you and maybe putting your side into the lead. And then you muff it—and, amidst jeers from opposing spectators, feel a proper Charley!

For a penalty-taker is really on a hiding to nothing. He's *expected* to score—and let's face it, he SHOULD score—so he doesn't get over-much credit when he does.

Apart, that is, from the relieved slaps-on-the-back from his own team-mates . . . the plaudits going mostly to the "underdog" standing apprehensively between the posts. And, what's more, rarely any of the blame if he fails.

Some players have always enjoyed the responsibility of taking penalties, but many is the star who's deliberately shied-off that chance of increasing his personal goal-tally.

One notable exception, of course, being Francis Lee—whose 33 First Division goals for Manchester City in 1971-72 included a record 13 penalties.

Latterly, though, things have changed a bit—with a European competition tie-breaking rules having put a new dimension into the job.

For, once "in Europe", every player—goalkeepers included—has to be prepared to step up confidently and take a vital spot-kick which might well decide who goes forward to the next round.

Consider the unhappy fate of Allan Hunter in Ipswich's UEFA Cup Quarter-Final in the spring of 1974.

He'd played a real blinder throughout both legs against Lokomotiv Leipzig—the 1-0 home win, and the 0-1 away defeat—when, with the aggregate-score level and no away goals to count double, the penalty tie-break came into operation.

Poor Allan, immaculate in everything else he'd done, missed out sadly on his own turn at the penalty-spot—and Ipswich were out.

Much the same sort of thing happened—though, this time, with a happier ending—the following season when Derby met Atletico Madrid in the same competiton. But then it was the English club who were spot-on on the spot.

Promotion Settler

After a great fight-back in Madrid, Derby were level-pegging at the end of normal play—following up a 2-2 result at home with an identical scoreline away.

So off they all went on the penalty caper. After the regulation five shots a side, each team had muffed one—which meant they had to continue, alternately, till one or other side missed again.

It got to 7-6 to Derby when Eusebio—who perhaps lacked the cool of his great Portuguese namesake—was set to level matters, but didn't quite angle his shot wide enough of Colin Boulton's left.

Somehow the Derby 'keeper bravely and brilliantly finger-tipped the penalty-shot against the post—and safely clear—and, amidst great scenes of Derby jubilation, the English side were through.

When it comes to Leeds . . . now there's a side which surely has the edge in the art of penalty-taking.

Few players can "place" them more accurately than Johnny Giles, nor "blast" them more fiercely than Peter Lorimer. When he has to take the job himself, skipper Billy Bremner's no slouch at it, either.

But, when it comes to sheer coolness, you've just got to hand it to Allan Clarke.

Amidst the tension of a crucial World Cup game in Mexico, "Sniffer" calmly slotted home a vital penalty against Czechoslovakia to give England a narrow 1-0 win to see them through to the Quarter-Finals.

And it was in his very first full international, at that!

MOST PENALTIES SCORED IN A SINGLE LEAGUE SEASON—13 by Francis Lee (Manchester City; Div. I; 1971-72). 11 by Willie Hall (Spurs; Div. II; 1932-33) and John Ball (Sheffield Wednesday; Div. I; 1932-33). 10 by Tom Callendar (Gateshead; Div. III North; 1949-50), John Evans (Southend; Div. III South; 1921-22), and Peter Morris (Mansfield; Div. III; 1966-67).

FRANNIE LEE . . . on the spot for Manchester City against Leicester.

Players are on the SPOT

MOST PENALTIES SCORED IN CONSECUTIVE LEAGUE GAMES—3 by George Johnston (Cardiff; Div. II; 1965-66) and Willie Cook (Everton; Div. I; 1938-39). (Cook's goals were scored in four days over Christmas—on 24th, 26th, and 27th December).

PETER LORIMER . . . makes it 4-0 for Leeds against Sheffield United.

MOST PENALTIES SCORED IN A FIRST DIVISION GAME—3 by Billy Walker (Aston Villa v. Bradford City; November 1921), Charlie Mitten (Manchester United v. Aston Villa; March 1950), and Ken Barnes (Manchester City v. Everton; December 1957).

MOST PENALTIES SAVED IN A LEAGUE GAME—3 by William Scott (Grimsby v. Burnley; Div. II; February 1909).

when they take this KICK

MOST PENALTIES MISSED IN A LEAGUE GAME—3 by Manchester City (v. Newcastle; Div. I; January 1912), and by Burnley (v. Grimsby; Div. II; February 1909).

GOALKEEPERS SCORING PENALTIES—In 1923-24, in Div. III North, Arnold Birch scored five penalties for Chesterfield; a record for any goalkeeper in the Football League.

Since the F.A. Cup Final moved to Wembley in 1923, there have been only four penalties—all of them successful—though the first, in 1938, was undoubtedly the most dramatic.

With the score still 0-0, and a replay looking certain, Preston's George Mutch was heftily brought down in the area by Huddersfield's Alf Young in the last 30 seconds of extra time.

But Mutch picked himself up, dusted himself down—and coolly cracked home the spot-shot which sent the Cup to Preston.

By an odd coincidence, the same two teams had also met in the last pre-Wembley match of 1922, when similarly a penalty—the first ever actually to decide a Final—provided the only goal of the game.

The one difference—on that earlier occasion, the penalty was *for* Huddersfield, and *against* Preston!

A penalty has also played a vital part in the fate of the League Championship—and, at the other end of the First Division table, in relegation, too. In their final match of the 1923-24 season, a missed spot-kick against Birmingham cost Cardiff the title when play ended in a goal-less draw.

Instead, the Welshmen—who'd never before, or since, won the title—had to be content with runners-up spot on goal-average.

"Headed" Penalties

Similarly, in Manchester City's last game in 1925-26, a penalty save by the Newcastle's 'keeper sunk City to a 2-3 defeat—when a draw would have saved them from relegation to the Second Division.

Both those vital penalties were fairly straightforward ones—but two of England's greatest and most famous pre-war players are amongst the five men who've actually HEADED a goal as a split-second reflex-action from their own penalty-kick.

"Trendsetter" in this trick was full-back Eddie Hapgood—who performed it for Arsenal against Liverpool in January 1935—followed by "Dixie" Dean for Everton against West Bromwich in the November of the following year.

What happened, of course, was that the desperate 'keepers punched the ball dead-straight back to the spot-kicker for a second go with his head instead of a boot.

In his long career, "Dixie" Dean scored 349 League goals for Everton—more than any other Englishman for a single club—but he certainly never got another chance for one of *that* kind!

The two players involved in the last incident of this nature, by the way, are still around in the game—Dave Simmons, then playing for Bournemouth, who headed home the penalty punch-out of Jimmy Cumbes (then Tranmere) in a Third Division game in January 1969.

Another kind of bizarre penalty episode took place in October 1945, when six times the Partick Thistle goalkeeper saved a spot-kick against Kilmarnock—and each time the referee ordered it to be re-taken because he judged the 'keeper had moved too soon.

He then, made a SEVENTH save—which, to his profound relief, the ref. ruled as legitimate.

That most-taken penalty was just one of the hundreds of thousands awarded since the spot-kick law was adopted on the mainland of Britain—the Irish F.A. had actually introduced it a year earlier—at the start of the fourth Football League season of 1891-92.

And the first player here to score in the League from the dreaded spot?

A certain Joe Heath earned himself that little niche in football history when, playing for Wolves on 14th September 1891, he successfully plonked one home past the Accrington 'keeper.

Iain Phillip
Dundee

East or West, Alan's best

1974/75 was a mixed season for Alan West. The former Burnley star was back in Division One action with Luton Town, which more than made up for the disappointment of a transfer to Sunderland falling through on medical grounds. A pity for Alan that The Hatters found life "upstairs" such a strain, but the young schemer's form was most impressive.

3 stars recall THEIR FIRST

'Kidnapped — and held to ransom'

BY WILLIE MATHIESON (GLASGOW RANGERS)

WILLIE is a tough, uncompromising, talented defender.

But as he looks back to his first big game in the club's blue shirt, he thinks it is marvellous that he didn't fluff his professional career right there and then.

For strange things happened in the week that saw his debut in the senior side. A mixture of drama and comedy. It was in 1965, and Willie was picked for his first game in a home Scottish FA Cup game against Hamilton Academicals.

He says: "A really big break, especially coming after 18 months with reserve sides. The atmosphere of the Cup . . . tremendous! If you don't let it get on top of you, you've just GOT to enjoy it.

Charity

"In fact, I had a good game, and we won 3-0. As easy as the score suggests, and I found I was able to adapt to the pace of senior football. That was a good sign. I was so desperate to make the grade, but it's only normal to have a few doubts.

"Manager Scott Symon had a special word with me, told me what I should look out for, added that team-mate Jimmy Miller would be keeping a special eye open for me. But eventually I adapted myself to the terrific change of atmosphere . . .

"Cup day in Glasgow was always the students' charity day. And when they're out in search of money, almost anything can happen. The first thing they did was nick the match ball . . . all the balls in fact. So we didn't even get a kick-around before the match began.

Drama

"Perhaps the comedy of the situation helped me settle down so well. But the drama was on earlier in the week. There was I, with the Rangers' first-team squad, training for the big Saturday ahead. And this bus turned up at the training ground. Out jumped a load of students . . . and they then jumped me, and two other players. Before we knew just what was happening . . . we'd been kidnapped!

"And those lads would not release us until the club had agreed to let the students collect for their charity at the game on the Saturday. Afterwards it sank in that it was all a bit of a giggle, but at the time I wondered just what WAS happening!"

Willie (right) was once kidnapped by students — and held to ransom!

'So nervous, I couldn't tie my bootlaces'

PHIL PARKES (Q.P.R.)

WHEN Queens Park Rangers goalkeeper Phil Parkes played his First Big Match as a professional, he was just a bag of nerves, so scared he couldn't even tie up his bootlaces.

He says: "It's true . . . I had to ask one of the apprentices to tie the laces! But it was the whole atmosphere of this game, when I was with Walsall, back in 1969.

"It was a home game against Mansfield. I'd signed with Walsall as an amateur, then turned pro, got stuck in the reserves. But with around eight matches in the Third Division left, we were really struggling.

So Fast

"So me, the new boy, got a call-up, and everybody expected something special to stop the rot. Once I'd got my laces fixed, the real troubles started out there on the park.

"Maybe you've heard how a new goalkeeper, or a substitute keeper, is always brought into the game as soon as possible, to give him a feel of the ball. Not with me. No early pass-backs to boost my confidence. The other lads were just as short on confidence in me as I was in me, so they felt they couldn't risk even a gentle tap of a backpass.

"And I figured my first-team career was over early on, when Mansfield came through and scored. Everything seemed to be happening so fast—I know there wasn't time to try and think things out. But . . . we went on to win 3-1, a vital win. It was a real turning point for the club that season and we kept on winning through to the end of the season and relegation ended up quite a few points away.

"Our manager, Bill Moore, told me afterwards that he was very pleased with me, that he felt I had a real future in the game, and boosted me a bit more by keeping me in the side all the way through. Next season, too, before I was transferred to QPR.

"You remember little things about the first big one—little things are important. Me—I'd been an apprentice carpenter, working just a few miles from Fellows Park in Walsall. And on that first-team debut, fifty or sixty of my old workmates turned up to give me vocal support. That was really great for the new boy."

Q.P.R. 'keeper Phil Parkes was very nervous on his debut for Walsall.

BIG GAME

'We lost—but I won promotion to the First Division'

BY LARRY LLOYD (COVENTRY)

THE year: 1969. The place Bristol Rovers' homely Eastville ground. The occasion: Fifth Round of the FA Cup . . . Third Division Rovers against mighty Everton.

Rovers had done well to get that far. A home win over those Cup-fighters Peterborough, a win against Kettering, a real away upset against Bolton Wanderers.

And playing outstandingly well at the heart of the Rovers defence was Larry Lloyd, a raw-boned sixfooter who positively exuded class and determination even in the Third Division.

Stirring

That game against Everton was to prove his first REAL big match. Says Larry: "It'd be great for me to make it a fairy-story, say we beat the mighty Merseysiders out of sight. In fact, we lost by the only goal of the afternoon. But even so it was a fair old game, and we produced some stirring stuff for our fans.

"My man was Joe Royle, playing very well. He'd knocked in more than 20 goals that season, and everyone was saying he'd be an England regular and once in would be hard to dislodge. I wasn't short of advice on how to cope with him, but talking is different from DOING, when you're out there on the park.

"We had a pep talk from our manager, Freddie Ford. He told us it was a big game for us, but it was also a big game for Everton, too. He said not to worry, they're just a load of kids. Joking, of course . . . and Joe Royle didn't look much like a kid to me. But it was a matter of building confidence.

"In fairness to me, I did do well. Royle is good in the air, but I was getting my fair share of the high balls. All the same, we lost. No hiding the disappointment, because the club had only twice before got through to the Sixth Round of the FA Cup."

But sitting in the stand, taking a very close interest in the big defender was one Bill Shankly, manager of Liverpool. Apart from his delight at seeing his Merseyside rivals given such a close game, he was even happier with the form of Larry Lloyd. In a few weeks, Larry was a Liverpool player—and Rovers were some £50,000 better off through the transfer fee.

Says Larry now: "Funny thing is that I'd always had a lot of time for Everton. I'd watched them a lot on television, admired the way they played. But it really would have been something if we'd knocked them out . . ."

Go For The Double Answers

Across:
(1) John Hickton. (6) Nag. (7) Brady. (10) Oar. (11) It. (13) Nibs. (15) Parkin. (17) Gnu. (18) St. (20) Clark. (22) Dino. (26) Fir. (27) Porterfield.
Down:
(1) Jennings. (2) Hugh. (3) Ibrox Park. (4) Kid. (5) Of. (8) York. (9) Brentford. (12) Tin. (14) Butler. (16) Is. (19) Fife. (21) Roe. (23) Nil. (24) Up. (25) If.
Jumbled Name: JOHN CRAGGS.

Score A Soccer Century Answers

1. Billy Jennings. 2. False (Domarski scored it). 3. Fifteen points. 4. He appeared as a substitute and scored the only goal of the game. 5. Johnny Hart, who, a few months later, was forced to retire because of ill health. 6. Colin Bell. 7. Rangers and Hibernian. 8. Front row-third from the left. 9. Tommy Langley. 10. Two-Swindon won 3-1, after extra-time.

Crossword Answers

Across
1. Relic. 4. Morrissey. 9. The Wolves. 10. Obese. 11. East. 12. Storm. 13. Head. 16. Home tie. 18. Evanson. 20. Milkins. 22. Bremner. 23. Glue. 24. Court. 25. Isle. 28. Aston. 29. Telescope. 30. Tony Parry. 31. Dates.
Down
1. Rotherham. 2. Leeds. 3. Coop. 4. McVitie. 5. Reserve. 6. Idol. 7. Stevenson. 8. Yield. 14. Stein. 15. James. 17. Mel Sutton. 19. Nerveless. 21. Spotter. 22. Burnley. 23. Giant. 26 Snap. 27. Used.

Carlisle United goalkeeper Allan Ross is under pressure . . . but he manages to fist this Middlesbrough attack away to safety.